The Urban Challenge in Education

The Urban Challenge in Education

The Story of Charter School Successes in Los Angeles

Joseph Scollo,
Dona Stevens,
and Ellen Pomella

ROWMAN & LITTLEFIELD
Lanham • Boulder • New York • London

Published by Rowman & Littlefield
A wholly owned subsidiary of The Rowman & Littlefield Publishing Group, Inc.
4501 Forbes Boulevard, Suite 200, Lanham, Maryland 20706
www.rowman.com

Unit A, Whitacre Mews, 26-34 Stannary Street, London SE11 4AB

Copyright © 2015 by Joseph Scollo, Dona Stevens, and Ellen Pomella

All rights reserved. No part of this book may be reproduced in any form or by any electronic or mechanical means, including information storage and retrieval systems, without written permission from the publisher, except by a reviewer who may quote passages in a review.

British Library Cataloguing in Publication Information Available

Library of Congress Cataloging-in-Publication Data
Scollo, Joseph.
  The urban challenge in education : the story of charter school successes in Los Angeles / Joseph Scollo, Donna Stevens, and Ellen Pomella.
      pages cm
  Includes bibliographical references and index.
  ISBN 978-1-4758-1443-9 (cloth) — ISBN 978-1-4758-1444-6 (pbk) — ISBN 978-1-4758-1445-3 (electronic) 1. Charter schools—California—Los Angeles. 2. Education, Urban—California—Los Angeles. 3. Educational equalization—California—Los Angeles. I. Title.
  LB2806.36.S36 2014
  371.05—dc23   2014025045

Contents

Acknowledgments   vii

Preface   ix

Introduction   xiii

Acronyms   xix

Prologue   xxi

Part I—Charter Elementary Schools

1 Fenton Avenue Charter School   3
   Lake View Terrace, California

2 Antonio Maria Lugo Charter Academy   15
   Huntington Park, California

3 Milagro Charter School   23
   Los Angeles, California

4 Synergy Charter Academy   33
   Los Angeles, California

Part II—Charter Middle Schools

5 Lakeview Charter Academy   47
   Lake View Terrace, California

6 Valor Academy Middle School   57
   Arleta, California

	7	View Park Preparatory Charter School *Los Angeles, California*	67

Part III—Charter High Schools

	8	Bright Star Academy *Los Angeles, California*	77
	9	Environmental Science and Technology High School *Los Angeles, California*	87
	10	Dr. Olga Mohan High School *Los Angeles, California*	97
	11	Port of Los Angeles High School *San Pedro, California*	107

Part IV—Charter Span Schools

	12	Camino Nuevo Charter Academy *Los Angeles, California*	119
	13	Gabriella Charter School *Los Angeles, California*	129
	14	Larchmont Charter School *Los Angeles, California*	139
	15	Magnolia Science Academy *Reseda, California*	149
	16	Our Community School *Chatsworth, California*	159
	17	Vaughn Next Century Learning Center *Pacoima, California*	169

Conclusion	181
References	185
Index	187
About the Authors	201

Acknowledgments

There are so many people to thank for making this book possible. To begin with I would like to express my appreciation to the school leaders, principals, teachers, staff, parents, and students of the charter schools listed in this anthology. Each of them exhibited tremendous pride in their school, and an openness and willingness to share their school story. Their passion and belief in charter schools was self-evident as we discussed their trials and tribulations of opening a charter school in Los Angeles. With people such as these, there is no doubt that the charter school movement in L.A. will continue to grow and prosper.

I'd like to pay special tribute to two of my colleagues at California State University Dominguez Hills. Ann Chlebicki, executive director of the Charter and Autonomous School Leadership Academy (CASLA) at CSUDH, and Toni Issa Lahera, codirector of CASLA. It was because of Ann's hard work and leadership that we received a grant from the U.S. Department of Education's Office of School Leadership to develop and implement CASLA, which made the funding for this book possible. And, of course, Toni, whose boundless energy, enthusiasm, and knowledge kept us moving forward to reach the goals of CASLA.

I also would like to express how fortunate I was to be able to work with my two coauthors on this book, Dona Stevens and Ellen Pomella. Both Dona and Ellen spent many hours researching each school's story by analyzing and reviewing data and meeting with school representatives in person, by e-mail, and on the telephone. I am deeply indebted to them for their tireless efforts and dedication to the project.

Several of my colleagues read early portions of this book and offered comments and suggestions. As we neared completion of the manuscript, Toni Issa Lahera and Keith Myatt reviewed the final draft and provided cogent and valuable feedback to improve it. Their assistance was very much appreciated.

I am also most grateful to all of the staff at Rowman & Littlefield for their assistance with the publication of this book, in particular Tom Koerner, vice president for education. He advocated for the book and offered sage advice to improve the quality and readability of the manuscript.

Finally, I'd like to thank my wife, Lynn, and daughters, Suzanne and Stephanie, for their love and support—listening and encouraging me in all of my endeavors over the years.

—Joseph Scollo

Preface

This book is an outgrowth of a grant that was awarded to the College of Education (COE) California State University Dominguez Hills (CSUDH) from the United States Department of Education (USDOE) School Leadership program in August 2010. The grant, Charter and Autonomous School Leadership Academy (CASLA), was developed and written by a team of educators under the leadership of Ann Chlebicki, who was the chief writer, principal investigator, and executive director; Antonia Issa Lahera and Joseph Scollo also served as writers and codirectors of the project.

With the implementation of CASLA it was discovered there was very little written about charter schools in the western part of the United States. We were alarmed to find out that little had been written about charters in California—the second state in the nation to enact charter school legislation, which currently has more authorized charter schools than any other state and has been a leader in educational reform. We were equally surprised that also missing from the literature was a discussion of the charter school movement in Los Angeles, a city where over 130,000 students attend charter schools.

Since the 1960s Los Angeles has been on the vanguard of the nation's efforts to improve public education and eliminate the achievement gap. The Los Angeles Unified School District (LAUSD) enrolls more than 640,000 students in grades kindergarten through twelfth grade, at over 900 schools, and nearly 250 public charter schools. The boundaries spread over 720 square miles and include the megacity of Los Angeles as well as all or parts of thirty-one smaller municipalities plus several unincorporated sections of Southern California (Los Angeles Unified School District, n.d.).

In recent years there has been an explosion in the development and establishment of charter schools throughout the United States. Because of L.A.'s diversity and size it is important to study the expansion of the charter school movement there. The school portraits in this book provide critical lessons about seventeen highly successful charter schools: urban schools that are making a difference in the lives of the students and communities that they serve. The lessons learned from these schools can be extrapolated and serve as a blueprint for current and future charter school operators throughout the country.

CASLA emerged over a two-year period of research based on lessons learned from a previous grant that was awarded to the COE in 2008 by the USDOE. The Urban School Leaders (USL) program was a project designed to train future school leaders in high-poverty, low-performing urban schools in the LAUSD. It was an innovative program focused on training school leaders to create learning communities in identified schools to improve student achievement.

In working with USL candidates, principals, and other stakeholders, a need was recognized to create a unique training curriculum and delivery method for the ever-growing number of charter and autonomous school leaders. CASLA's design is based on research and best national practices on what charter and autonomous school leaders need to know and be able to do to effectively lead and turn around urban schools.

There are over 250 charter schools currently operating within the attendance boundaries of the LAUSD, with approximately 130,000 students enrolled. As you can imagine, it was difficult to select schools to be highlighted in this book. As we looked at the variety of charters in Los Angeles, we realized we could not possibly include all the many fine and deserving schools that exemplified the criteria that were set. We wanted to be sure we included representative schools from all areas of the city, including different levels (elementary, middle, high, and span schools), organizational models (independent and affiliated), and curriculum types (thematic and nonthematic).

In addition to the above guidelines, the following criteria were used when selecting schools: (1) evidence of continuous academic growth and/or an Academic Performance Index (API) of 800 or above; (2)

evidence of a stable school environment; and (3) evidence of strong leadership and collaboration with the school community. Once the list of schools was established, many, many hours were spent interviewing key personnel, and researching data before schools were selected.

The California Department of Education (CDE) website provides a wealth of data to the public. The data to be used were narrowed into categories over a three-year period: ethnicity, socioeconomic status, English learners (EL), Students with Disabilities (SWD), Academic Performance Index (API), English language arts (ELA), and mathematics. All data were the most current data available for the year indicated. In some instances we could not locate the percent of ELs for the 2010–2011 academic year. In all other instances the percent of ELs was determined by the EL report to the CDE.

The charter school movement is dynamic and ever changing. Some of the leaders you will encounter here have moved onto other positions, but the schools you will read about continue to demonstrate a high level of academic performance and success. This anthology endeavors to share a snapshot in time of seventeen highly successful charter schools in Los Angeles. As you read these vignettes you will meet a group of educational pioneers who are passionate about charter schools and their value to public education.

Introduction

The Los Angeles Unified School District (LAUSD) is a large urban school district that stretches over 720 square miles, a public school system of enormous size. It is a school system that serves some of the poorest children in the nation and also meets the needs of some of the most successful students in the nation. Witness the recent winning of this year's United States Academic Decathlon. In fact, L.A. schools have more Academic Decathlon winners than any other school district in the country. Indeed, Los Angeles schools are a study in contrasts.

In recent years Los Angeles schools have experimented with a number of educational reform movements. Since the passage of charter school legislation in California, the expansion of charter schools has grown exponentially in Los Angeles. It now has one of the largest groupings of charters in the nation.

This book provides readers the opportunity to deeply examine seventeen highly successful charter schools. It documents the trials and tribulations that each school faced at its formation, the impetus that led to the development and implementation, the practices that contributed to their success, and their hopes and dreams for the future of their school. Each of these schools exhibits a passion for excellence led by a dedicated principal/director, a committed staff, and a supportive community.

Organized into six parts, as well as this introduction, the book is intended to provide a basis for understanding the charter school movement in Los Angeles and its implications for public school systems in the country. It is arranged by school level, which allows the reader to compare and contrast the similarities and differences of the schools featured.

Introduction   Provides the reader with the purpose, and a short summary of each part of the book.

Prologue   A brief historical perspective of recent major educational reform efforts in Los Angeles is discussed. This provides the context for the reader to understand what transpired in Los Angeles to lead to the significant growth of charter schools.

Part I—Charter Elementary Schools   This part of the book discusses four unique elementary charter schools located in different areas of Los Angeles. Fenton is located in Lake View Terrace; Antonio Maria Lugo in Huntington Park; Milagro in Lincoln Heights; and Synergy is in Watts.

Fenton and Synergy are independent charters that were started by two very different, yet dynamic, leaders. Fenton was established in 1993 and became the second conversion charter, the seventh charter school in LAUSD, and the thirtieth charter in the state. As a conversion school it faced challenges not associated with a start-up charter. Synergy opened its doors as a charter in 2004 with 104 students, and since has grown to be a most successful charter.

Antonio Maria Lugo and Milagro are also start-up charters, however, they were started by charter management organizations. Lugo was founded in 2005 as the flagship for Aspire Public Schools in Los Angeles. Aspire began as a charter management organization in 1998 with the goal of becoming a pathway for underserved California students. Its main offices are in Oakland, and it has grown to serving over thirty-four schools in California and Tennessee.

Milagro is one of thirteen charter schools managed by the Partnerships to Uplift Communities (PUC), a nonprofit serving Los Angeles and the San Fernando Valley. Their small public charter schools work to uplift and revitalize communities through the development of educational and other supportive partnerships.

Part II—Charter Middle Schools   Middle schools bridge the gap between elementary and high schools. There are not many middle schools in the charter world. Many elementary schools have expanded their curriculum to meet the needs of the middle school student, while others have created span schools to cover a variety of grade-level configurations. Lakeview Charter Academy is located in Lake View

Terrace; Valor Academy Middle School is in Arleta; and View Park Preparatory Charter Middle School is in South Central Los Angeles.

Lakeview was founded by two visionary leaders in 2004. Both Jacqueline Elliot and Ref Rodriguez had a common mission to improve secondary students' achievement in densely populated urban areas plagued by low achievement and high dropout rates. As you read the story of Lakeview, you will discover that the mission of Drs. Elliot and Rodriguez was definitely achieved.

The founder of Valor, Hrag Hamalian's, personal experience served as an impetus and inspiration for its establishment. As a young Teach for America teacher he was assigned to teach at a troubled high school in Los Angeles. While there he became disillusioned with the abysmal graduation rate and even worse rate of graduates matriculating to college. At the age of twenty-two he determined he would start a charter school from scratch. Valor opened its doors to the Arleta community in 2009 and since then has gone on to become a very successful middle school.

The third middle school highlighted is View Park Prep. It is one of the thirteen schools managed by the Inner City Education Foundation (ICEF), all located in South Los Angeles serving students from underperforming public schools. ICEF was founded in 1994 by Michael Piscal, who left his position teaching English at Harvard-Westlake School, one of the nation's top private schools, with a vision of bringing that same high-quality education to disadvantaged children in urban Los Angeles. View Park has become a flagship for ICEF and is a true success story.

Part III—Charter High Schools Four charter high schools' stories are shared in this book. Two of the four are operated by the Alliance for College Ready Public Schools, and the other two are independently operated high schools. Of the four schools two are thematic based. All of the schools are start-up schools.

Bright Star was founded by Jeff Hilger, a former attorney and Teach for America teacher. As a fairly new school, Bright Star Secondary Academy has garnered numerous awards including Number One Performing Charter School in LAUSD (California Charter Schools Association, 2008), California Title I Distinguished School Award (California Department of Education, 2009), and California Distinguished School Award (California Department of Education, 2011).

Environmental Science and Technology (ESAT) High School and Dr. Olga Mohan High School are operated by the Alliance for College Ready Public Schools. The veteran LAUSD educators who created the Alliance brought forth this successful school model in part through the strong partnerships they established over time with the community and Los Angeles business. The LAUSD school reform movements of the 1990s seem to be fully realized in this and other Alliance schools throughout Los Angeles.

The last of the high schools featured is the Port of Los Angeles High School (POLAHS). Like ESAT, POLAHS has a thematic-based curriculum centered on maritime studies and international business. The school is the result of San Pedro business leaders and educators working together to create a highly successful entrepreneurial high school. The school opened in 2005 with 112 ninth graders, and has grown to over 950 grade nine through twelve students. As with many of the schools in the book, POLAHS has also received several well-deserved awards and grants.

Part IV—Charter Span Schools   Span schools are common in the charter school world.

Most span schools were developed from existing elementary schools, and some from existing high schools. Six successful span schools are shared in the book, three located in Los Angeles: Camino Nuevo Charter Academy, Gabriella Charter School, and Larchmont Charter School. Magnolia Science Academy is located in Reseda, Our Community in Chatsworth, and Vaughn Next Century Learning Center is in Pacoima.

Four of the schools have a kindergarten through grade eight organizational structure: Camino, Gabriella, Larchmont, and Our Community. Magnolia has a grade six through twelve configuration, and Vaughn has a prekindergarten through grade twelve structure. Only two of the schools are operated by a charter management organization: Camino Nuevo and Magnolia; the remaining four are all independently operated, with Vaughn being the only conversion charter school. Two of the span schools are themed based: Magnolia focuses on science, and Gabriella's theme is dance.

Perhaps the most unique of these schools is Vaughn. Vaughn is a conversion school that has expanded from an elementary school to a prekindergarten through grade twelve, and plans are underway to expand this configuration to a prekindergarten through grade sixteen campus.

Conclusion Summarizes the seventeen vignettes by drawing from them seven lessons learned from these successful schools. These lessons learned are essential elements that are present and common among all of these exceptional charter schools.

As you read these school portraits, you will see that each portrait has six sections: Introduction, Data Implications, Success Factors, Conclusions, Future Plans, and Key Elements.

Introduction Provides the background and context for the development of the school. It discusses their goals and vision for the school. It explains the motivation for establishing the school, and the challenges that were encountered.

Data Implications Shares with the reader the most current data available. It analyzes the school's performance on the Academic Performance Index (API) and Adequate Yearly Progress (AYP). It compares and contrasts some performance results with those adjacent similar schools.

Success Factors In this section the reader will meet a variety of different people, such as a teacher or staff member, parent or community member, and/or business or university partner. Each will give opinions about the school and why it is such a success. The principal/director, along with teachers, will highlight and discuss successful practices and programs that are used at the school that contribute to its success.

Conclusion A brief summary of the school's portrait is shared with the reader, oftentimes with some final remarks by the school's teachers, parents, or principal.

Future Plans No doubt as you read this book you will find that the leaders in these schools are dynamic people. They are always looking forward. Their plans may consist of adopting a new mathematics program, implementing a new curriculum, or expanding or establishing another charter school. This section shares the dreams of the staff and school.

Key Elements At the end of each vignette you will find a bulleted list of elements that are evident in these successful schools. These key elements enable these schools to meet the needs of their students, and achieve exceptional results. They are elements that can be replicated in other schools throughout the nation. But it is not easy: It takes a great deal of dedication, hard work, and commitment.

The schools in this study had to deal with difficult decisions and challenges to be successful. They faced a multitude of dilemmas, but their success was well worth it.

Acronyms

A-G	Approved high school A-G courses are required for Admittance to the University of California and the California State University system
AMO	Annual Measurable Objectives
AP	Advanced Placement Courses
API	Academic Performance Index
AYP	Adequate Yearly Progress
CAHSEE	California High School Exit Examination
CMO	Charter Management Organization
CST	California Standards Test
CSUDH	California State University Dominguez Hills
CSUN	California State University Northridge
EL	English Learner
ELA	English Language Arts
ELAC	English Language Advisory Council
ELD	English Language Development
IEP	Individualized Education Plan
KIPP	Knowledge is Power Program
LAAMP	Los Angeles Annenberg Metropolitan Project
LAUSD	Los Angeles Unified School District
LEARN	Los Angeles Educational Alliance for Restructuring Now
LMU	Loyola Marymount University
MOCA	Museum of Contemporary Art
PREP	Prepared, Respectful, Engaged, and Professional
SAT	Scholastic Aptitude Test
SDAIE	Specially Designed Academic Instruction in English
SST	Student Study Team
STAR	Standardized Testing and Reporting
STEM	Science Technology Engineering and Math

SWD	Students with Disabilities
TCRP	The College Readiness Promise
UCLA	University of California Los Angeles
USC	University of Southern California
WASC	Western Association of Schools and Colleges

Prologue
A Historical Perspective

The publication of *A Nation at Risk: The Imperative for Educational Reform*, a report on the status of public education in the United States, was published in 1983. The report surveys various studies that point to academic underachievement of students on national and international scales (National Commission on Excellence in Education, 1983). It served as a lightning rod for a series of educational reforms throughout the country that continue to this day. A central theme of one of the reforms is to provide parents with more options in the public school system. This, along with other factors, helped to influence the development of the charter school movement.

In 1991 Minnesota passed the first charter school legislation in the nation, and shortly after, in 1992, opened its first charter school, City Academy High School, with an enrollment of thirty students (City Academy High School, n.d.). Currently Minnesota has 146 charter schools in operation serving more than 39,000 students (Minnesota Department of Education, 2013). Presently forty states and the District of Columbia have enacted charter school legislation.

On September 22, 1992, California became the second state in the nation to pass a charter school law. The intent was to allow for the creation of schools that operate independently from the existing school district structure. The purpose of the law is to:

- Improve student learning.
- Increase learning opportunities for all pupils, with special emphasis on expanded learning experiences for pupils who are identified as academically low achieving.

- Encourage the use of different innovative teaching methods.
- Create new professional opportunities for teachers, including the opportunity to be responsible for the learning program at the school site.
- Provide parents and pupils with expanded choices in the types of educational opportunities that are available within the public school system.
- Hold the schools established accountable for meeting measurable pupil outcomes and provide schools with a method to change from rule-based accountability systems.
- Provide vigorous competition within the public school system to stimulate continual improvements in all public schools (Kerchner, Menefee-Libey, Mulfinger & Clayton, 2008).

After two decades of offering school choice to families, the charter school movement in California has spurred the creation of 1,065 of the nation's 6,000 charter schools. The growth, moreover, has been explosive: Nationwide, one in five of the new public charter schools that opened last year was based in California. Statewide, the number of charter schools has doubled every five years. (Center on Educational Governance, 2013, p. 1).

Prior to the passage of charter school legislation in California, a consistent set of reforms began to emerge in LAUSD. Generally these reforms centered on universal high standards, decentralization, greater parental and grassroots engagement, and variety and choice in types of schooling (Kerchner et al., 2008).

The teacher strike of 1989 touched off a wave of governance reforms that changed the way schools did business in Los Angeles. When the nine-day strike ended in late May, many were relieved; however, with its end came new challenges. Among other things that were included in the negotiated settlement of the strike was a provision for school-based management (SBM) and shared-decision making (SDM) councils to be established at every school site (Clayton, 2008). The district began to implement decentralization and local school sites began to have limited authority over five key areas that affected school operations: (a) staff development program; (b) student discipline guidelines and code of student conduct; (c) schedule of school activities and events, and special schedules; (d) guidelines for the use of school equipment, including the copy machine; and (e) control of selected budgetary accounts.

The LEARN (Los Angeles Educational Alliance for Restructuring Now) plan was approved by the LAUSD Board of Education in spring 1993. LEARN was a nonprofit coalition of business, civic, and education leaders. It was committed to creating a fundamentally different educational system, a new institution (Kerchner et al., 2008). LEARN's efforts were guided by four principles: (a) decentralization with accountability, (b) collaboration, (c) school-site action plan, and (d) professional development (Ouchi, 1999).

Shortly after LEARN was approved, publisher Walter Annenberg announced a gift of $500 million to public education in the United States. This challenge gift generated more than $600 million in matching grants and thus targeted more than $1.1 billion for education reform. The Annenberg challenge in Los Angeles was known as LAAMP (Los Angeles Annenberg Metropolitan Project).

The initial idea was to get LAAMP to work closely with the existing LEARN project, and "go broader and deeper." One of the LEARN ideas that had largely gone unrealized was creating groups or clusters of schools that would operate together so that school autonomy would be joined with a decentralized operating system. So, the LAAMP plan was built around what was called "school families," each comprised of a high school and its feeder schools (Kerchner et al., 2008).

Both LEARN and LAAMP were ambitious plans to create institutional change in LAUSD. However, as these plans were being implemented throughout the system, there were political events and administrative decisions that impeded the success of these plans, i.e., changes in the makeup of the board of education, changes in superintendents, and the reorganization of the district. In addition, there were external political influences that impacted the district, such as the election of a new mayor.

These programs were beneficial to the district and many are "still using the ideas, frameworks, practices, tools for collaboration, etc. In many places it was a failed reform because people didn't get beyond the governance issues into the transformation of instructional practice" (Kerchner et al., 2008, p. 163).

Perhaps one of the most important resolutions the board of education passed in 2009 was Public School Choice (PSC). It had a significant impact on the growth of charter schools in LAUSD. The PSC initiative was a landmark reform for LAUSD. By allowing alternative operators—whether charter school organizations, the mayor, or groups of teachers—to apply to manage scores of new and low-performing schools, it set the standard for putting students first.

The theory was that anyone could apply and the very best applications would win, ensuring that students attended the best-run schools the district could offer. Just as important, charter operators in the program would have to accept all students within each school's enrollment area rather than using a lottery system under which more motivated families tend to apply for charter schools (Staff, 2011).

As LEARN and LAAMP came to an end in 2000, many of the people who were active in LEARN found themselves organizing or running charter schools. While LEARN sputtered, the charter school movement expanded rapidly in Los Angeles (Kerchner et al., 2008). There are two types of charter schools: conversion and start-up.

- A conversion charter is a school that converted from a traditional public school into a charter school.
- A start-up is a charter school that is created organically, without converting from an existing school.

These charters can be fully independent of the district or district-affiliated, which have closer ties to the district. Both must have their charter proposal approved by the board and both are held to a high level of accountability.

LAUSD has more students enrolled in charter schools than any other U.S. school district. Over 130,000 students are enrolled in over 250 charters, or about one in every six students district-wide. The following vignettes are representative examples of the many fine charter schools in Los Angeles that are changing the face of public education there and throughout the nation.

Part I

CHARTER ELEMENTARY SCHOOLS

CHAPTER 1

Fenton Avenue Charter School
Lake View Terrace, California

INTRODUCTION

Eighteen years ago Fenton Elementary School was plagued by issues that kept its students performing at the single-digit level on standardized tests. Teachers were dissatisfied with LAUSD for myriad reasons. They had just suffered a 10 percent pay cut. The staff was divided along the lines of bilingual versus nonbilingual teachers. There was a feeling that Fenton was a "dumping ground" for unsuccessful staff from LAUSD, and that the site was being neglected as funds were poured into other areas of the district.

The school was located in a low socioeconomic area with a high crime rate, a great deal of graffiti, and it had a reputation for having tough kids. Teachers recall that it was impossible to get substitute teachers because they were afraid to come to Fenton. Yvette King-Berg, who was the coordinator of the school at the time, recalls that boxes of math books would arrive at the school unordered and unneeded. Personnel at central LAUSD were making decisions that had little or nothing to do with the school's needs. There was an overwhelming feeling that the money being generated by Fenton students was not being spent on Fenton students, and that LAUSD was hindering their ability to serve children.

Two dynamic leaders are given credit for bringing everyone together. Principal Joe Lucente and Assistant Principal Irene Sumida were convinced that they could unify the school by building a charter. When holding discussions about the vision for this new and exciting possibility of self-determination, it became clear that once the charter was approved, the kids in the neighborhood were not going to change; what needed to change were the staff's expectations and their ability to dream that they could do something amazing, and that the kids could rise to that level of expectation. The mantra of the teachers became, "We want to build a school that we would want even our own children to attend." (That has become the case.)

In 1993, Fenton became the second conversion charter, the seventh charter school in LAUSD, and the thirtieth charter school in the state. Most of the other charter schools were start-ups. Being a conversion charter presented more difficulty because the staff was unionized and used to the practices in LAUSD. Although going independent was a big stretch for many of the staff, they had implicit trust in their leadership and their ability to ensure that Fenton was on the right path to create an environment conducive to student success. After the vote was taken to become a charter school, only two staff members decided to leave (one teacher and one custodian).

Being a conversion school meant that Fenton's attendance area remained the same and that their student population has remained stable with approximately 60 percent of their enrollment from the neighborhood and 40 percent from outside the attendance boundaries. All students are welcomed. No lottery has been necessary because Fenton has remained on a year-round calendar, enabling them to carry a larger enrollment. Neighborhood students have priority, then out-of-attendance-boundary students are accepted to the school's capacity and a wait list is developed.

Writing the charter petition allowed staff to take ownership of issues and move away from the excuses of "we can't because" to "we will in spite of." Freed from union constraints, teachers took on additional responsibilities and started spending more hours preparing their classrooms and working with students before, during, and after school without additional pay. Since the control of resources and budget was at the school site instead of at the district level, staff could identify the supports and training needed, and decide to spend their resources specifically targeting defined areas of need.

The language of the original petition addressed the bilingual issue that had divided the staff. The fact that English was not the students' first language was no longer accepted as an excuse for lack of achieve-

Data Implications

Year	Enrollment	% AI	% Asian/Filipino/ Pacific Islander	% Black	% Hispanic	% White
			Ethnicity			
2012–13	653	0.2	3.7	7.0	88.0	1.2
2011–12	941	0.1	2.8	6.2	89.9	0.5
2010–11	943	0.2	2.2	6.4	90.0	1.0

Year	% Socioeconomic	% English Learners	% Students w/ Disabilities
2012–13	96.8	25.3	13.3
2011–12	88.0	37.9	12.4
2010–11	87.4		10.2

Year	API	% AYP—English Lang Arts*	% Mathematics*
2012–13	808	47.3	63.9
2011–12	815	52.1	65.1
2010–11	804	48.7	64.7

* = Percent at/above Proficient

ment. The approval of the charter petition written by the staff gave them a sense of synergy and a oneness of mind that they were a team that had to work collaboratively to utilize the strengths and skills of each teacher.

In 2012 Fenton separated into two schools: a primary center and an elementary school serving grades three through five, now having an enrollment of 653 students. Of these students, 88 percent are Hispanic, 7 percent are African American, and 5 percent other ethnicities. All students participate in the Free and Reduced-Price Lunch Program (reported as Socioeconomically Disadvantaged by the CDE). ELs comprise 25 percent while SWDs comprise 13 percent.

The staff at Fenton is extremely proud of their gains in the state's API. In 1999 the school's API was 473. Over the last thirteen years, their API has grown by 342 points to their current API of 815. Every year saw gains, with the exception of 2005, which saw a drop of 19 points from 710 to 691. This was the same year that Fenton entered Program Improvement Year 1.

The school met sixteen out of seventeen of their Annual Measurable Objectives (AMOs), but the EL subgroup failed to meet the target of

24.4 proficient and advanced in ELA. According to Dr. David Riddick, Fenton's director, "Our staff is extremely reflective and very good about looking in the mirror and looking in one another's eyes—and instead of coming up with excuses, they come up with ideas to attack challenges that we face."

To address the area of concern with EL proficiency, the staff came together to develop strategies to attack the problem. Explicit language instruction, *Thinking Maps*, access to the core curriculum through visual and nonlinguistic representation, and other proven strategies such as think-pair-share were embraced and implemented. In the 2006/2007 and 2007/2008 school years, the school met all of their AMOs and was able to exit Program Improvement.

Although growing in their API scores in the school years 2008/2009, 2009/2010, and 2010/2011 by 57 points, Fenton once again found itself in Program Improvement, based on the African American, Hispanic, EL, and Socially Disadvantaged subgroups' scores in ELA and mathematics. A thorough examination of their data and that willingness to be reflective has served the staff well. For the 2011/2012 school year, Fenton met all seventeen of their AMOs through Safe Harbor. Safe Harbor is an alternative method for meeting AMOs by showing progress in moving students from scoring at the below-proficient level to the proficient level.

SUCCESS FACTORS

When the first charter was approved, every single staff member had a voice and a vote to determine Fenton's course of action. The governance model at the school has changed over the years, but essentially the same tenet holds true: All staff are responsible and held accountable for the decisions at the school. Every full-time staff member (certificated and classified) sits on one of the four governing councils. Participation is a nonnegotiable condition of employment. These councils oversee business, finance, school/community relations, curriculum, assessment, and human resources.

In addition, much like union stewardship there are faculty representatives who bring to administration the concerns of the staff. Leadership is distributed to all staff at all levels of the organization from the directors to the plant manager; therefore they are heavily invested in everything that happens at the school. Teachers especially feel more in control because they are asked their opinions on how things are run and how funds are allocated and expended.

Early on the decision was made to spend the majority of funding on personnel who interact directly with students. In addition to classroom teachers, there are other personnel that serve the students. Fenton students have instructional specialists who teach art, music, science, and physical education. Teacher assistants provide extra support to students. Very few of the resources go to administration, which consists of a director and assistant director. Recently, when budget cuts had to be made, cutting music, art, science, or physical education teachers was never considered. Rather than cut these essential services for students, the teachers took a 5 percent pay cut.

This governance system of self-empowerment applies to the hiring and firing of personnel. There is a rigorous process to hire new teachers, which includes an application process, intensive screening, an essay, key questions, a résumé, an interview, and presenting demonstration lessons. Currently the teaching staff is very stable—no one has been hired in the last four years.

The process for selecting administration is equally rigorous. When Fenton converted to a charter, Joe Lucente and Irene Sumida transitioned from the traditional principal and assistant principal of the school to codirectors. With Lucente's retirement five years ago (he remains on the board of directors), Irene Sumida became director. Sumida retired about two years ago from her paid position; however, she continues to be involved in the school as the unpaid executive director.

Dr. David Riddick was selected as the new director for grades three through five. He recalls that Irene Sumida told him his first week on the job, "Give away all the credit, and take away all the blame." In addition, she gave the administrators, front office staff, and support staff a rock that says GAMAN. Roughly translated, it means "Suck it up." Regardless of what the issue is, take ownership of it and find a way to get it done. The rock is a symbol of steadfastness and personal responsibility that are unique to Fenton.

The right to terminate personnel is another factor that has allowed Fenton to develop its excellent, committed teaching staff. At the time of the conversion, there were some staff members who had been placed at Fenton, some of whom did not meet the high standards set for the new charter school. The process for termination started with a peer assistance plan that provided help through a colleague /grade-level chair or lead teacher and spelled out specific goals for improvement.

Typically when that didn't work, the teacher would either retire or leave. Others went back to LAUSD. Dr. Riddick has not had to terminate anyone because, as he puts it, "The staff that's here right now is unbelievable. The other director and I have been given the keys to a Ferrari."

Focused and strategic professional development has played an important role in Fenton's success. Every Wednesday is an early release day, and one day a month, on Wednesday, the students are dismissed at noon. In addition, the teachers have collaborative planning by grade level twice a week during psychomotor time. At Fenton, there is a laser-like focus on data. A combination of different summative and formative assessments is examined at the school level, then by grade level, then at the individual teacher level. Using these analyses, goals are set for the school, for the grade level, and for the individual teacher. This is done during professional development as well as goal-setting meetings when the director meets individually with each teacher.

Assessment results are regularly reviewed, and any discrepancies in how the teacher's students performed in comparison to other classes are noted and discussed. Taking the analysis further, five ELA CST clusters are examined (word analysis, written conventions, reading comprehension, writing strategies, and literary responses). Word analysis and written conventions are identified as the most essential for higher-level thinking and became a focus of intervention time.

They also look at cognitive strategies that the students need and focus on presenting the information in a meaningful way so the students have a personal connection to it. For example, professional development on similarities and differences as a metacognitive technique to help the student's brain comprehend and store information for immediate recall became a priority. Graphic representations, visual nonlinguistic forms of instruction for students such as *Thinking Maps* are also studied and used school-wide. The professional development used Marzano and colleagues' (2001) *Classroom Instruction That Works*. Professional development is driven by what the data reveal teachers need to do collectively as a grade level and individually.

This is the first year of a full inclusion model for all special education students. Nineteen special day class (SDC) students, including autistic and emotionally disturbed students, are now fully included in general education classes. The two SDC teachers are working collaboratively with the resource specialist teacher (RST) in a push in / pull out program based on the students' specific needs. Three of the nineteen are struggling, and the staff is weighing different options on the best way to serve these children.

While this new model has presented challenges, Dr. Riddick is pleased with the implementation of full inclusion in the school. He stated, "Our goal is to keep all our kids—we don't want to send any away. We own this. If it's our issue, we want to keep the kids here and do whatever we can." Further he stated, "To be selfish about it, if you can't figure out a way to solve these problems, you're never going to grow your staff. If your motto is 'We get rid of problems,' then you're never going to deal with the problems and you're never going to find ways to tackle difficult situations." As one of the teachers stated, "We need to get better—it isn't that we want to get the kids out—we need to improve."

One of the SDC students was struggling. Rather than simply look for another placement, a tiered approach was outlined to try before that extreme solution was used. The student could have a more intensive behavior implementation plan, the student's schedule could be adjusted to get more support from the RST, a behavior specialist could be hired to train the whole staff, or as a final resort an alternative placement could be explored.

Fenton does not use special programs for special-education students, English learners, or gifted students. Rather, students are provided a differentiated instructional program based on their unique needs as defined by rigorous data analysis. A tiered intervention/enrichment program enhances students' access to the core curriculum. There is specific time in the day when teachers work with individuals depending on their needs. Some grade levels split students up so that one teacher may work with students who need extra help. The other teacher then may work with students with higher-level thinking skills (regardless of having been identified as gifted) by challenging the students with research assignments or projects.

Regardless of label, all students receive support through technology such as *I-Station*. *I-Station* is used during intervention time and gives the students guidance in areas of deficit and provides specific lessons for the students to use during intervention. Students who are advanced are given lessons that challenge them. Instead of limiting explicit language-development instruction and visual and nonlinguistic representations pedagogy to the English learners, all students benefit from this kind of instruction. The elements of Response to Intervention (RtI) are utilized—data-driven instruction, progress monitoring, and tiered intervention/acceleration.

At the time when the charter petition was developed, there was much discussion about the technological divide. Fenton had no computers in the classroom and most Fenton families did not have access to computers. The staff adopted a technology plan that provided a computer for every child based on the philosophy that if Fenton students couldn't go to all the amazing places that privileged families had the opportunity to send their kids to learn about the world, technology could be a way to equalize that playing field. Enough computers were purchased to provide a computer for every upper-grade student and three to eight computers for each primary classroom.

All teacher workstations connect to a ceiling-mounted video projection unit that projects the teacher's laptop, document camera, DVD or VCR player onto a retractable screen, accessible through a switch at the teacher station. There is a voice amplification system in every classroom, which includes a wireless headset for the teacher and handheld microphone for student use. Teachers have found this especially effective with English learners as the projection system makes things close up and zoomed in. The raised station/microphone clarifies and amplifies the teacher's voice so that students have a much easier time understanding the lessons.

One underpinning of Fenton's success is the attention to the social/emotional growth of their students. Many students come from very challenging circumstances. There are children from the projects and homeless shelters; many children are from single-parent homes. The neighborhood suffers from gang violence and shoot-outs. At the core of Fenton's mission is to build the capacity of the students to feel safe in the school.

A great deal of team building is done—not only teacher to student, but also student to student. *Discipline with Dignity* is part of the culture of the school. Every action is based on respect for the child—no child is ever belittled. When behavior issues arise, students are given choices on how to handle the problem. The teacher handles the problem in a dignified and tactful manner. Teachers make contracts in the class, so if students do something, they know the consequences and then are given choices to make amends. The goal is to empower the students so that when they come to school, they know they are respected.

A full-time school counselor is funded in order to work with the most at-risk students. The counselor has an assistant named Jeter who assists in teaching children crucial social and emotional skills through the *Mutt-i-grees* program. This curriculum, developed by the Pet Savers foundation in collaboration with Yale School of the 21st Century, strives to help children become more kind, caring, and compassionate to their friends, families, and animals. Jeter is a shelter dog who works at school each day to help implement lessons in which children learn critical skills that will help them in school, at home, and later in the workplace, and with their interactions with people and, of course, with animals.

FUTURE PLANS

Fenton has remained on a year-round schedule in order to accommodate the number of students who want to attend, and they have made the best of their year-round status by offering intersession to students whenever they are off track. A major goal is to acquire a second site so that the school can have its primary center (K–2) on one site and its elementary school (3–5) on another site. This will allow them to go to a traditional calendar while at the same time maintain their enrollment. Although research supports small traditional campuses, Fenton is very proud that it has outperformed all other schools in the area in spite of their size and traditional calendar status.

A future goal has been discussed to create a Fenton Middle School. Parents are concerned about the education their students will receive when they leave Fenton. They have become accustomed to the high expectations set for their children, and their high success rates. The students at the middle schools their students would attend are performing at very low levels, and private schools are not an option for these families. Beyond middle school, Fenton High School is another dream.

Dr. Riddick expressed a goal to work more collaboratively with LAUSD because there are so many things that could be shared and learned from each other. He stated, "We're all here to do the same thing—we should be allies. We're not at war—it's really a war on poverty. The more time we spend fighting one another, the less time we can service the kids that really need our help."

CONCLUSIONS

Eighteen years ago two dynamic leaders knew that things had to change for the students at Fenton. The dream of creating a place that put the needs of children first and empowered staff to make that vision a reality has endured and flourished. As teacher Stacey Hutter put it, "You can't become a Fenton in a year. This has been a lot of work. It's a long process that started out with two people who knew why it needed to change and they sold it. All the rest of us were invited on board and helped, but they always give credit to us. They set the tone for professionalism, the vision, and brought people of like mind along. Our staff is incredibly hard working. There are no lazy butts here!"

Dr. Riddick sums it up in three simple words. "We own it! We like to think of ourselves as an Ellis Island approach—regardless of what your need is, we're going to find a way to systematically address your particular area of strength and area of need."

Distributive leadership through inclusive governance ensures that every member of the school community shares the responsibility and accountability for every aspect of the school. Students' academic, emotional, and social success is the basis for every decision made. Students receive a rigorous education grounded in the state standards. High expectations are set for them, and they rise to those expectations. They receive a well-rounded education that does not forsake art, music, and science, and . . . they have Jeter!

KEY ELEMENTS

- A powerful and purposeful vision that is shared by all, including staff, teachers, administrators, students, parents, and the community.
- Shared decision-making is practiced. All staff are held accountable for the decisions at the school.
- Distributive leadership is evident. Leadership is distributed to all staff at all levels of the organization from the director to the plant manager.
- Data are constantly being analyzed and used to improve the level of student achievement.
- Focused and strategic professional development is conducted regularly to improve the skills of all, including teachers, staff, and parents.

CHAPTER 2

Antonio Maria Lugo Charter Academy
Huntington Park, California

INTRODUCTION

Huntington Park calls itself "The City of Perfect Balance," thirty square miles of business and industry existing alongside suburban housing in this southeast area of Los Angeles County. When first established in 1906, it had a population of 526 residents that has since grown to over 58,000, while many of the factories and businesses that peaked mid-century have declined or closed. By the 1990s, the mostly white population of Huntington Park had left the area to move south to newer Orange County suburbs, and that vacuum filled with Latinos from East L.A. and recent immigrants from Mexico.

A drive down the main thoroughfare, Pacific Boulevard, reveals buildings that formerly housed major retailers, now home to discount stores, Mexican restaurants, and independent vendors. It is fitting that the Aspire Antonio Maria Lugo Charter Academy, located just off this main street, is named after the original family who received a land grant from the King of Spain in the late 1700s. By naming this successful charter school Antonio Maria Lugo, Aspire has tapped into the history of the people who settled the land and now reside there.

Aspire, whose main offices are located in Oakland, was founded as a charter management organization in 1998 with the goal of becoming a pathway for underserved California students to attain a "College for Certain" education. Aspire's mission, posted on an office wall of Aspire Antonio Maria Lugo Academy (AMLA), is "to open and operate small, high quality charter schools in low-income neighborhoods in order to increase the academic performance of underserved students, develop effective educators, share successful practices with other forward-thinking educators, and catalyze change in public schools."

From its first school in Stockton, Aspire has grown to thirty-four schools serving over twelve thousand students in six cities across the state. Not only do Aspire schools average an 820 API score, but 100 percent of its graduates gained admission to four-year colleges or universities. AMLA opened in 2005 as the flagship Aspire school for Los Angeles in Huntington Park.

Aspire's mission and vision are communicated and supported at AMLA as part of everyday conversations between teachers and teachers, teachers and students, and teachers and parents. All Aspire schools have morning meetings with the students where the principal shares announcements and the students participate in college cheers. These cheers encourage enthusiasm for the day ahead and make the direct connection between students' current schoolwork and future goals. The morning meeting is just one of Aspire's signature practices.

Aspire principals have a great deal of autonomy in their work. They are empowered to make sound decisions with the backing of the Aspire organization. There is constant communication between the home office and the site leaders with support from the area superintendent. Aspire handles the reports and much of the paperwork so principals can make instruction the first priority, visiting each classroom every day and having the time to plan and work closely with teachers.

At the site the principal utilizes a leadership team comprising the principal, lead teachers, and a literacy specialist to make many of the decisions guiding instruction and student achievement. "Purposefulness is one of Aspire's core values and it is played out in some of that decision making," states Dr. Roberta Benjamin, area superintendent of Aspire Los Angeles. There are some decisions that are not made at the site level and are made among principals or senior leadership, but there are opportunities for surveys and feedback so that decisions are very informed.

In Huntington Park, Aspire has opened four elementary schools, one middle school, and one high school. AMLA has an enrollment of 235 students K–6, compared to the thousand-plus attending each of the nearest LAUSD elementary schools, Middleton Street and Miles Avenue, both located within a few blocks of the Aspire school. With its API of

Data Implications

			Ethnicity			
Year	Enrollment	% AI	% Asian/Filipino/ Pacific Islander	% Black	% Hispanic	% White
2012–13	235	0.4	0	0	99.6	0
2011–12	234	0.4	0	0.4	99.1	0
2010–11	224	0.4	0	0.4	98.7	0

Year	% Socioeconomic	% English Learners	% Students w/ Disabilities
2012–13	96.6	45.1	13.2
2011–12	94.0	44.9	7.2
2010–11	97.3	62.0	7.8

Year	API	% AYP—English Lang Arts*	% Mathematics*
2012–13	835	62.2	70.7
2011–12	825	59.2	67.7
2010–11	847	64.7	74.0

* = Percent at/above Proficient

835, AMLA is above the Aspire average and surpasses the scores of Middleton at 778 and Miles at 782. Demographically, all three of these student populations are almost identical, with approximately 99 percent Hispanic and 96 percent or more Socioeconomically Disadvantaged. AMLA has an English-learner population of about 45 percent while the LAUSD schools average around 40 percent. Comparing AMLA's 2011 California Standards Tests (CST) to those from 2013, the school's proficient/advanced rate has dropped slightly in ELA and mathematics. The comparison of the 2013 scores of AMLA to those of its LAUSD counterparts shows that the Aspire school still has a better record overall. In ELA, AMLA scored an average of 62 percent proficient/advanced compared to Middleton at 47 percent and Miles at 45 percent, and in math AMLA's 70 percent average of proficient/advanced outshined that of Middleton at 62 percent and Miles at 57 percent.

The fact that most students at AMLA live in the surrounding neighborhood and that there are as many students on the wait list as are enrolled, proves that the community is well aware of the academic accomplishments of this school.

At Aspire, according to Dr. Benjamin, the curricular and instructional decisions emanate from data analysis, and not just large, formalized sets of data like the CST. The school uses the Cycle of Inquiry (COI), a process whereby teachers can assess what students know before instruction in order to tailor lessons to support that knowledge and build upon it. Teachers then administer a post-test to find out not only what the students know but also how effective their lesson design and implementation was. The COI lets the teachers use daily exit slips and other checks for understanding.

One of the reasons for the school's academic strength is its focus on data. Aspire schools are very responsive to what the various forms of assessment can show them about student progress. The Aspire schools network utilizes benchmarks that are administered at each school in the fall, winter, six weeks before the CSTs, and in the summer. There are several formalized opportunities for instructors to really look at how they have been doing by asking themselves, "Have I addressed all these standards?"

The powerful thing about the pre-CST is it really helps focus on what can be done six weeks prior to this big assessment and prioritize the standards to help students develop a greater sense of their own efficacy to do well on the CSTs. The results of these benchmarks are placed in a data portal, giving teachers a wide range of user-friendly reports to be used individually and in teacher teams.

Aspire assists the analysis of data at school sites through their training and support of Data Drivers (teachers who take on this extra duty in addition to their teaching responsibilities). "The Data Drivers are trained by our chief data analyst from Aspire's home office," explained Dr. Benjamin. "The teachers show other teachers how to use our data tools which are really comprehensive and very specific. We have an intranet data portal which is also connected to a teacher resource portal." Data Drivers bring teams together and provide professional development to help them go deeper into data analysis of student assessment results.

SUCCESS FACTORS

Aspire attributes the success of AMLA to the dedication of the teachers and staff. There are many factors that come into play and lead to success. "Our core values, customer service, collaboration, purposefulness—all come into the picture in concert with one another," states Dr. Benjamin. The teachers work incredibly hard because they know that coming into Aspire they will not be working in isolation.

All schools build a special schedule to allow for preparation time. During their preparation times and before and after school, teachers collaborate to plan objectives, write lessons, analyze data, and look at student work using protocols. AMLA's staff of nine teachers, a physical education teacher, literacy specialist, and special-education specialist works with students, parents, and each other to meet the goals of the school.

Due to the small size of the school, teachers must be creative. For instance, the literacy specialist works to infuse reading and writing instructional guidelines into lessons addressing science-content standards with an art outcome. The literacy intervention specialist is also responsible for the after-school program and is the main driver of the school's Response to Intervention program.

AMLA's curriculum is standards based and similar to all schools across Aspire. "We are excited because our schools that will open in Memphis next year are doing the Common Core," mentioned Dr. Benjamin. "It will be a great opportunity to learn from them and take some practical ideas back to our schools here in California." AMLA does not embrace a packaged curriculum, but rather uses the *Readers and Writers Workshop* methods of Lucy Calkins, adding different components through the years, but essentially keeping the same structure of a reading mini-lesson, a writing mini-lesson, and differentiated reading instruction through guided reading.

Some teachers work on the same schedule and organize students into guided reading groups so students will not have just one reading teacher. Students might go across the school into another reading group. Even the special science teacher works on incorporating reading into the science curriculum. The students see that reading happens all around, even with the physical education teacher.

In terms of textbooks and teaching strategies, Aspire schools tend to use many of the same resources. "We're looking at *Number Strings* across many of our sites as a way to build mental-math proficiency," stated Dr. Benjamin. She explained principals and other leaders use Aspire-wide meetings and trainings to present a resource or strategy that they feel others should replicate, a method that disperses new ideas quickly throughout their community.

"We are doing more with technology this year," according to Benjamin. "All teachers have an iPad that they can use not only for their own professional organization, but also for use with Apple TV, where they can screen video clips, or phonics exercises, or a writing app for their students." The classrooms all have computers for student use during workstation time.

Another success factor is the Aspire-wide strategy of what they call Student-Led Solution or SLS. "It's an opportunity for students to use academic language to discuss an academic idea and bring evidence to bear in this problem-solving strategy," explained Benjamin. This method is utilized from kindergarten through high school and is a key component to preparing students for success in college. "By the time they get into their higher grades, they know how to talk about their work," according to Benjamin. "They know what is expected of them."

AMLA's professional development program is ongoing and much of it occurs during the school day. Teams of teachers work together during their prep period or during times when students are in PE or with the science/literacy teacher. New hires receive a weeklong new-teacher training conducted by Aspire. All school sites participate in a retreat each year to focus their efforts on the needs of their school. Principals meet each summer to discuss the "must achieves" for the school year and what that looks like at each school site.

Because every Friday is a release day, teachers either meet on site or attend regional professional-development activities with other Aspire teachers. Some of the schools dedicate time to team building. At AMLA teachers have gone bowling together. Last year AMLA took a museum trip to the Museum of Contemporary Art (MOCA) and invited teammates from another Aspire school to join them.

Aspire is a member of The College-Ready Promise (TCRP), the Bill and Melinda Gates Foundation's program that promotes a staff evaluation system to improve teacher effectiveness and results in merit pay. With TCRP, Aspire's teachers have three informal observations connected to an Internet tool called The Purple Planet. The Purple Planet is a comprehensive data portal where observation data are recorded and teachers can access resources to improve their practice. Besides informal observations, each school is committed to doing at least one formal evaluation connected to The Purple Planet, which houses the data and the process itself.

In addition to effective teaching and standards-based curriculum, AMLA offers its students and families many support services. The school has had a partnership with California State University Los Angeles for their counseling intern program and Benjamin's connection with Loyola Marymount University (LMU) brings them master's students and other volunteers to help teachers. This year the school hired a full-time marriage and social worker counselor who works with students and hopes to engage more families.

AMLA additionally supports its students with a school-wide meeting first thing in the morning, followed by a school-spirit activity, and then breakfast before moving to their academics. To support a positive school culture, they have adopted the CARES model—Cooperation, Assertiveness, Responsibility, Empathy, and Self-Control—as a means to identify positive behavior actions and the academic vocabulary students need to describe their feelings. Twice a year the school invites parents to accompany their children to Saturday School, a chance for parents to experience a school day in the life of their child. Teachers lead workshops and even community groups participate to make this experience informative for parents. Each family makes the commitment to the school of thirty hours per child each year. Parents earn hours by attending school activities, workshops, meetings, conferences, fund-raising, and helping in the office and classrooms. Parents have expressed interest in literacy workshops, and health and wellness workshops on topics like drug use and violence in the community for this year's meetings, and the school staff will accommodate their requests.

FUTURE PLANS

This school year the growing number of students entering into Huntington Park's Aspire schools has caused AMLA to adjust. Instead of opening two kindergarten classrooms, the school only opened one and instead added one sixth-grade classroom. The reason for this decision was that the Aspire middle school, Centennial College Preparatory Academy did not have enough seats to accommodate their students. While there may not be a specific plan in place for opening more Aspire schools or increasing the number of seats at existing schools, it is clear that AMLA is dedicated to the community and will continue to provide an excellent education for its students. "We want to continue to serve Huntington Park," stated Benjamin. "Our plans involve providing consistency and stability." She wants the community to see the school not only as a place for excellent academics but also for the community "to find support and feel empowered to take this same important work and excellent outcomes to other schools and other communities."

CONCLUSIONS

Though AMLA is a small school, it serves as a model of what true educational insight and reform can look like. The close-knit administration, staff, faculty, and parents effectively work together to move each child forward to achieve social and academic goals embraced by all stakeholders. The community of Huntington Park is almost identical to many areas throughout the country, a place crowded with recent immigrants where seeming insurmountable obstacles have thwarted the attempts of most public schools.

AMLA has taken on the challenge and devised ways to overcome the obstacles of poverty and illiteracy. This school can truly catalyze change in the larger public school systems that surround it.

KEY ELEMENTS

- A dedicated and committed staff who are passionate about improving the academic performance of underserved students.
- A clearly defined set of core values that is supported by all: customer service, collaboration, and purposefulness.
- The extensive support and guidance from the charter management organization's home office.
- The use of data to drive the instructional program.
- Professional development that is flexible and conducted regularly to allow teachers to collaborate, plan objectives, write lessons, analyze data, and evaluate student work using a set of protocols.
- A school that is an integral part of the neighborhood and serves as a focal point for the community.

CHAPTER 3

Milagro Charter School
Los Angeles, California

INTRODUCTION

Northeast of Chinatown and west of Lincoln Heights, the 110, 101, and 5 freeways forge an industrial triangle where large trucks hauling massive shipping containers race along Main Street among the warehouses and factories. The nearby Los Angeles River and the Piggyback Rail Yard feeding Union Station make this gritty area of Los Angeles an unlikely place for a successful elementary school.

Inside the Milagro Charter School—this "miracle" school—one would never guess that the building once served as a union hall for electricians. Milagro is one of thirteen charter schools managed by the Partnerships to Uplift Communities (PUC), a nonprofit serving Los Angeles and the San Fernando Valley. Their small public charter schools work to "uplift and revitalize communities through the development of educational and other supportive partnerships," according to their mission statement.

Further, with their goal to place schools in densely populated urban communities and prepare students for college admission and college success, they work to facilitate school reform within LAUSD through a regional approach. PUC schools operate on three design principles first put into practice at the highly successful University Park Campus School, a partnership between Clark University and local community groups that opened in Worcester, Massachusetts', most impoverished area in 1997.

All PUC schools make three commitments to their students, their parents, and their communities: (1) more college graduates for the communities they serve; (2) academic proficiency for all students within four years; and (3) student commitment to uplift their community now and forever. By living these commitments, Milagro has become both a California Distinguished School and a Title I Achievement Award winner.

When Milagro's principal, Sascha Robinett, met Dr. Ref Rodriguez in 2002, he had already made a name for himself in the charter school world. Along with Dr. Jacqueline Elliot, Rodriguez opened the Community Charter Middle School in 1999, the first charter school approved by the Los Angeles Unified School District Board of Education. By 2004 Rodriguez and Elliot had formally created PUC, Inc., to manage its growing charter school network, and Rodriguez, Robinett, and teacher Martha Moran formed the nucleus of a group that opened Milagro.

PUC manages its charter schools with a board of directors and regional directors to provide support to their principals, handling payroll, facilities rental, human resources, and community partnerships, thereby freeing the principal and instructional leaders to focus on instruction. "We are autonomous and allowed to make our own decisions as to what's best for our kids," said Robinett. As for decisions made on site, the school uses a collaborative model. "We try to create a strategic risk-taking culture," she continued. "To be innovative, you have to be comfortable trying something new; you have to be comfortable with the idea of failure."

Robinett herself has worked for over nineteen years as a teacher, administrator, and a professional-development trainer for a national program. This experience, she said, gave her "insight into schools across the nation, to really know what instruction is and to establish a culture. You have to understand that teaching and learning is an art form; you need to practice that in depth before you are going to develop anything."

Of Milagro's 287 students, 97 percent are Hispanic, 1 percent African American, 1 percent Asian/Filipino/Pacific Islander, and less than 1 percent are White. Almost 24 percent are English learners, and nearly 90 percent are Socioeconomically Disadvantaged, making a comparison to neighboring schools difficult.

The closest LAUSD school, Albion Elementary, is a few blocks away but its demographics reveal a different story: 24 percent Asian,

Data Implications

Year	Enrollment	% AI	Ethnicity			
			% Asian/Filipino/ Pacific Islander	% Black	% Hispanic	% White
2012–13	287	0.3	1.0	0.7	97.2	0.3
2011–12	285	0.4	0.7	1.8	95.8	1.4
2010–11	277	0.4	1.1	1.4	95.7	1.1

Year	% Socioeconomic	% English Learners	% Students w/ Disabilities
2012–13	89.2	23.7	17.7
2011–12	89.8	23.5	20.4
2010–11	94.6	16.6	23.6

Year	API	% AYP—English Lang Arts*	% Mathematics*
2012–13	885	70.9	87.3
2011–12	894	74.2	84.9
2010–11	912	77.7	89.4

* = Percent at/above Proficient

74 percent Hispanic, 42 percent English learners, and 100 percent Socioeconomically Disadvantaged. Milagro's students come from both the surrounding neighborhoods and cities throughout Los Angeles.

According to Robinett, "Students come from various places, some as far as Pomona because their parents work in downtown Los Angeles." The closest similar LAUSD school is Allesandro Elementary, three miles away, and Milagro's data compare favorably. With an API of 885, Milagro far outpaces that of Allesandro at 824.

On the California Standards Tests for 2013, Milagro averaged 71 percent proficient/advanced in English language arts (ELA) and 87 percent in math, while Allesandro averaged 59 percent in ELA and 70 percent in math. The school has a high special-education population of 18 percent, with students' disabilities ranging from ADHD to autism. The school takes everyone who is chosen in the lottery and believes that its inclusion model is the best way to serve all students.

"Curricular and instructional decisions are made by using both quantitative and qualitative data," stated Robinett. Teachers use data from standardized tests and summative assessments given three times a year to govern their instructional decisions made for an inclusive classroom.

"Everything is differentiated. We don't do it in stations or changing assignments. We do train kids to do what we call their personal best." The school uses data to help children and parents understand where they are and where they need to go. "Our special ed students don't know they are special ed," she said. "They have no idea; they are all special. Everybody has a need, an individual need."

Moran continued, "They don't ask why a certain student is working with the aide. They just know that someone is there to help whoever needs it. They know that if somebody is getting help, it is because that's what that student needs at the moment. They see it as a natural thing."

The school works to help students understand that "fair" is not necessarily "equal" and that every student gets what he or she needs. "When our teachers work with the inclusion team," commented Moran, "they just don't talk about the special ed students; they also monitor those kids who are not working to their potential. The school's culture, not allowing any student to fail, is evident in the support every student receives."

"We consider the CSTs the floor of our achievement goals, not our ceiling," said Robinett. "We have kids who can score advanced that we know are not on grade level, and we have the other kids who are making tremendous progress, but on a test like that, if you have language or visual processing issues, that growth will not be apparent."

Formative assessment is done every day in the classroom. At the end of each unit, workshop teachers conduct a quick analysis of student work, in addition to conducting individual conferences and working with small groups. Teachers use these data to create intervention groups and weekly lesson plans. End-of-unit application projects and assessments are used to determine students' ability to individually meet grade-level standards. Monitoring students' growth and meeting the needs of each student is the backbone of Milagro's academic program.

SUCCESS FACTORS

Perhaps the biggest factor leading to the success of Milagro is its commitment to each student's success beyond the classroom. This valuing of the individual is evident in all aspects of the school, from instruction to assessment, parent interaction, and teacher selection and training. "Our students practice the habits of a scholar and are referred to as scholars rather than students. We want our students to understand that learning is a lifelong process, not just a set of skills," explained Robinett. "We are always looking at our role and the family's role in ensuring our mission becomes a reality for all students. We work in collaboration, knowing that each stakeholder brings essential perspectives and skills to the table."

Robinett and Moran believe that everyone has a part in the creation of scholars. "It is not based on a hierarchy. Everyone has something to give and all contributions are valued," said Robinett.

The creation of a highly effective curriculum has been a priority at Milagro. The school has utilized America's Choice in conjunction with the California State Standards, underscoring their firm belief in the strength of the Common Core national standards that has been long-standing. Now that forty-five states have adopted the Common Core, Robinett is excited about the increased focus on thinking and the opportunity it creates for new partnerships with schools across the nation.

She herself creates curriculum maps and feels she and Moran's chief role is as researcher and resource for their teachers. "A teacher shouldn't have to find resources," stated Robinett. "There are many bad resources out there and finding good ones is time consuming. Every year we revamp the curriculum maps based on what we've learned."

The school looks to the work of Lucy Calkins, Ellin Keene, literacy experts, and other "gurus," as they call them, for guidance and direction. Another authority whose influence has helped shape the school is Carol Dweck whose book *Mindset* asserts that children and adults can "grow" their intelligence through perseverance and hard work.

This theme is realized in the Readers, Writers, and Mathematicians Workshop, which has reading, writing, and math infused into the curriculum of science and social studies. Another success factor is their language-learning model that is based on the transformative language acquisition philosophy.

"We don't use the label 'English Learners,'" said Robinett. "We believe in bilingualism. Our bilingual students are considered to be our top students because they can think and work in two languages; that is a much higher cognitive level of processing information."

They feel the "EL" label has held students back and hasn't allowed them to progress, causing them to potentially drop out and not graduate. Robinett explained, "All Milagro's teachers are bilingual and are able to support students' learning in both English and Spanish. Although instruction is primarily in English, students are supported and assessed based on their individual academic language needs."

Speaking, writing, and listening skills are incorporated into all learning tasks to develop students' ability to express their understanding and share their opinions with a variety of audiences. Students are required to both learn and use academic language to communicate their thinking and understanding in all workshops.

Milagro teaches the Common Core curriculum through classroom libraries filled with fiction and nonfiction books, magazines, and articles, and not with textbooks. Many unit lessons feature author studies, and the school invests in quality literature, hoping to develop authentic literacy in their students through excellent materials and resources.

"We did not take Readers First money so we did not have to adopt Open Court or another program that focused on phonics," stated Robinett. "Milagro strives to fill in the gaps in learning and bring all students to higher levels of reading comprehension. The reading-development methodology used at Milagro strives to help students understand from the beginning that we read for meaning."

"We have students coming from other schools who were told they were reading at or above grade level, thinking of fluency, but they were not comprehending what they were reading," stated Moran. "Teachers work to help students become metacognitive about their reading process through modeling, think alouds, conferencing, daily reflection, and goal setting." Students who struggle to meet grade-level reading standards are provided both small group and individual interventions before and after school, during class, and, if needed, are supported by the inclusion team.

Classrooms at Milagro are set up to maximize student interaction. They sit in collaborative groups because the school views education as a social process. "Rituals, routines, and artifacts are consistent from kindergarten except that the complexity is upped every year. We learn by thinking and thinking has to be visible," said Robinett.

"There are multiple forms of making thinking visible—Post-it notes, graphic organizers, response journals, peer and class discussions, and individual conferences." There are no bulletin boards in the classrooms; the only student work on the walls is student current writing, and this is posted to show that writing is a process.

According to Robinett and Moran, these examples serve to show students where they are and where they need to go. "We don't believe in just posting student work because it becomes like a museum," commented the principal. "Everything on the wall has to be a resource for kids and they are trained to use those resources. They are called anchor charts and teaching charts; there are no premade materials in a Milagro classroom."

In kindergarten, for instance, before a letter goes up on the wall, students study it, truly understand it, and one student becomes the leader for that letter, the expert. After the first two weeks of school all twenty-six letters are posted by the students and those letters become authentic resources for their study of words and their meanings.

The school guides the direction of instruction through professional development, which is the product of collaboration between leadership and teachers. Using evidence from classroom observations and data analysis of student assessments, the staff identifies areas of need and then develops its summer, midyear, and Thursday professional development programs.

Teachers work both as a staff and as grade-level teams "to check where we are with this, where we need to grow, how do we reach our goals," said Robinett. "We spend our last PD [professional development] Thursdays to deeply analyze and reflect on the year in order to create new goals for the following year."

Teachers meet regularly with either Moran or Robinett, who serve as instructional coaches. Teachers are also influenced by the school's partnership with the Pasadena Armory Art Center, which works with students and teachers to help them connect content to art and to think in metaphorical ways, something only an artist can bring, according to Robinett.

Careful teacher selection helps ensure a staff with like-minded professionals. PUC's human resource department manages the initial screening and then the school sends out an extensive questionnaire. Candidates teach a demonstration lesson and are then interviewed by a panel of teachers and administrators.

"Once we take somebody in," said Moran, "we take it as our responsibility to help them. It's a full commitment by all of us and that's why our turnover is so small." Teachers are expected to provide excellent instruction and monitor and support all learners. In addition, they engage in lengthy parent conferences running from one to two hours each in the fall and meet with parents as often as is needed to support student achievement. Very few teachers have fallen short of the expectations of the job.

PUC schools are part of The College Ready Promise, funded by the Bill and Melinda Gates Foundation. The emphasis on teacher and student growth using a uniform rubric fits in well with the Milagro mindset, but linking these criteria with compensation does not. "What we would like to see is bringing that money into the classroom," said Robinett. She feels that all teachers deserve bonuses and that everyone is an equal shareholder in the success of the school. She and Moran work hard to protect their teachers' passion for their work and always try to see the situation through that lens.

Finally, the parents of Milagro students are actively engaged in their children's education. The school does not ask for a set number of hours from parents who work in a co-op model. Parents are invited to participate in fund-raising, helping with school events and field trips, and parent workshops as well as the extensive parent conferences.

"We've tried several iterations of parent leadership groups," stated Robinett. "We are definitely in process." The school has its School Site Council and holds Milagro Family Meetings every other month, where parent-education topics are presented. Parents are invited every Thursday to read, share, or teach students during the first twenty minutes of instruction, and twice a year families participate in completing learning tasks that demonstrate how students learn within their classrooms.

The Lincoln Heights Neighborhood Council has been a supporter of the school, funding a nonfiction library and mats for physical education. The school has also been adopted by the Los Angeles Department of Water and Power.

FUTURE PLANS

Like most successful schools, the challenge is to maintain and even surpass past accomplishments. As Moran summed it up, "We are constantly learning, we are constantly building and doing away with what doesn't work, building on our successes. It takes time and you need to give it that time." Both Moran and Robinett feel that innovation is key to ensuring that their students continue to get the best, and it is through detailed analysis and reflection that the school will continue to progress.

The school has set a goal to increase the use of technology in their classrooms. Not all classrooms have document readers or LCD projectors, let alone computers for their students. "We just recently got netbooks because our laptops died; no funding has come in for technology," said Robinett. She is hopeful that the school will acquire the needed technology in the near future to accommodate the online assessments that the Common Core standards will bring. With the resolve and dedication of its leadership and teachers, Milagro will continue to move forward as a model to emulate.

CONCLUSIONS

This school has become a major success at providing an excellent education for an underserved student population by keeping their eye on the mission of the school. They have utilized the few resources available to them and efficiently and thoughtfully supported quality instruction as their top priority. From kindergarten on, students are considered scholars and families are important partners in the creation of these lifelong learners.

Milagro is truly a "miracle" school. The dedicated administration and staff have worked together to maximize the effect of their support for students and their families. The single-minded devotion to the school's mission has created this "miracle" for the community.

KEY ELEMENTS

- Ongoing, systematic assessment of student performance, the data of which drive immediate intervention and weekly lesson planning.
- A laser-like focus on each individual student's needs, both academic and social, and a collaborative approach to finding ways to meet those needs.
- A school culture that values creativity and innovations.
- An organizational structure that takes most operational decisions away from the school site so that administrators and other staff can work primarily to support instruction.
- A strong partnership with parents and families.

CHAPTER 4

Synergy Charter Academy
Los Angeles, California

INTRODUCTION

The founders of the Synergy Academies, Meg and Randy Palisoc, did not start their careers as K–12 educators. Mr. Palisoc came from a business background, studying entrepreneurship at the University of Southern California (USC), and working in an office after graduation. He became a teacher after visiting a college friend's classroom and being inspired to enter the education field.

Mrs. Palisoc, who also studied at USC, found a position in higher education working with college students at the USC School of Engineering. She says that both of them decided to become teachers because, "We had a mission and passion to change the world. I had a heart for the inner city and saw the disparity in the education those students were getting while kids from other places were getting a great education."

While both of them were seeing good things happening in their own classrooms, those student achievement gains were not seen in every classroom. They began to explore ways to make a greater impact for inner-city children. Mr. Palisoc attended an EL conference and attended a session entitled "Parent Choice." He came back excited and empowered. The couple applied for a start-up grant and wrote the application while teaching full time. Receiving only the first installment for $50,000 of the $450,000 grant, they took out a line of credit on their house to pay the teachers while they waited for the remainder of the funds to arrive.

The school opened in 2004 with 120 students in grades kindergarten through fifth. The first location was in a church selected because it was in a high-density area that had schools that were overcrowded, year-round, and the lowest performing in the district. The Palisocs stood on the street corner after work to pass out flyers about their new school; presentations were held at the church and the YMCA to build credibility with parents. At the first meeting, there were five parents; eventually, there was standing room only.

The church was a less than ideal location. There was no heat or air conditioning. The Synergy office had to be packed up every day, and the classrooms had to be packed up every week. After six years at the church location, Synergy was able to move to its current location as a colocator with Quincy Jones Elementary School in South Los Angeles, a brand-new school that opened up as a Public School Choice school.

Responding to the need for a logical matriculation pattern for their students, the Palisocs opened a middle school that grew to 480 seats (Synergy Kinetic Academy), and a high school that grew to 600 seats (Synergy Quantum Academy). All three schools emphasize science, technology, engineering, and mathematics (STEM). At the elementary level, the emphasis is on the use of technology to improve reading and mathematics skills. There is a waiting list of 370 students for grades kindergarten through fifth; the school currently operates at capacity with classes no larger than a 26:1 ratio.

The ethnic breakdown of Synergy's 311 students is 96 percent Hispanic, 4 percent African American, and less than 1 percent White. Approximately 53 percent of the students are on the Free and Reduced-Price Lunch Program (Socioeconomically Disadvantaged), 43 percent are ELs, and 13 percent are SWDs. Synergy's API rose from 709 in 2004/2005 to 907 in 2012/2013. The school met thirteen of thirteen AYP goals, and remains free of No Child Left Behind Program Improvement status.

There is a strong commitment to ensure that parents are fully aware of the school's testing data. As Principal Jennifer Epps shares, "Most parents don't know what an API is—what AYP is—that there's state testing in May. Our first year out we had an API of 709 and we were ecstatic that we'd gone over 700. Then we really looked at the stats to see that only 28 percent of our students were reading at grade level. We easily could have presented to the parents this fantastic 709—highest

Data Implications

Year	Enrollment	% AI	% Asian/Filipino/ Pacific Islander	% Black	% Hispanic	% White
			Ethnicity			
2012–13	311	0	0	3.5	95.5	0.6
2011–12	311	0	0	2.9	96.1	0.6
2010–11	311	0	0	5.5	93.6	0.6

Year	% Socioeconomic	% English Learners	% Students w/ Disabilities
2012–13	53.4	42.8	12.9
2011–12	91.3	44.4	11.8
2010–11	92.9		9.9

Year	API	% AYP—English Lang Arts*	% Mathematics*
2012–13	907	74.6	89.1
2011–12	934	84.2	92.6
2010–11	887	69.0	91.0

* = Percent at/above Proficient

in the neighborhood—highest in Local District 5—and rolled right on. The parents would have been as happy as can be. But we didn't. We shared everything with them and then told them what we were going to do next year." Every year Mr. Palisoc makes a data presentation for parents and staff that fully explains the scores, what they really mean, and what needs to happen next.

The first day of the All-Synergy professional development before school starts each year is always devoted to data analysis. Teachers use the time to brainstorm why certain subgroups progress and others do not and create their yearly plan to submit to the principal. In addition, Ms. Epps has one-on-one discussions with teachers around their students' scores.

Intervention is offered to students who are struggling; content is determined by the data and time of the year. Computer programs are used to support all students in basic skills, and the intervention becomes more grade-level specific closer to the CSTs. Intervention is also provided by the principal during the day. She pulls small groups of students who need individual attention. Her office is housed in the computer lab where she has a view of the yard and can monitor students' activities there as well as students' progress in the lab.

SUCCESS FACTORS

Synergy's reading and math strategies are collectively called Power Over Words, and Power Over Numbers, which are terms coined by Mr. Palisoc. Open Court was the adopted reading series for grades kindergarten through third (the school will be implementing a new curriculum for Common Core), and phonics cards are in every classroom, kindergarten through grade five. Convinced that Open Court is not rigorous enough, students write every day using Step Up to Writing. Kindergarten students are writing dictation by November.

In addition, students are taught with supplemental lessons in prosody, phonemic awareness, phonics, fluency, vocabulary, and reading comprehension. Believing that "big words aren't just for big people," teachers use larger vocabulary words with the students and work on multisyllabic words. Ms. Epps sums it up as, "Learning to read, reading to learn. People are always learning how to read and should always be reading to learn. Even the highest readers will come across words they don't know if they don't have the context. So, in the upper grades, we do syllabication, phrasing and dictation."

A major component in Synergy's success in reading achievement may be attributed to Reading Counts (Scholastic). Starting in second grade, students take a test that identifies their Lexile levels, and they must read books at that level and pass computer-based comprehension tests at the 80 percent or better level. Students in grades two and three are in the lab every day taking the quizzes; fourth and fifth grades are in the lab twice a week. The word-count goals are as follows:

Second grade	7,576/week	250,000/year
Third grade	11,364/week	375,000/year
Fourth grade	15,152/week	500,000/year
Fifth grade	18,939/week	625,000/year

Students who meet their word-count goals and do not fail any quizzes that week get an extra free-play recess from 2:00 to 2:25 p.m. A report goes home to parents every Tuesday to keep them informed about how well their students are doing in Reading Counts. At the end of the year, all students who have met their goals receive a medal.

Students who read a million words by the end of the fifth grade join the Millionaire's Club and are taken to a fancy lunch or dinner (to be treated like a millionaire!). In addition to Reading Counts, students participate in other supplemental computer-based reading programs. All kindergarten through third-grade students work in Ticket To Read, a phonics-based program, and grades four and five work in ReadAbout to read nonfiction.

The end goal behind Synergy's reading strategies is to empower students to be able to read and understand anything that is presented to them. This way, students will be able to engage in higher-level thinking, converse in higher-level discourse, and produce higher-level projects.

Synergy's mathematics strategies are collectively called Power Over Numbers. The basic core math text is published by Saxon (the school will be adopting new curriculum for Common Core), but is supplemented with a variety of manipulatives and other resources including teacher-developed materials. As Ms. Epps puts it, "We believe in old-school skill and drill! Students must know their [grade-level] math facts by the end of January." The reason for this is because Synergy has found that students struggle with mastering higher-level concepts and constructing their own learning in meaningful ways if they do not have a strong foundation from which to draw.

However, Synergy does not just teach its students to memorize math facts. Synergy believes in teaching a well-rounded curriculum that incorporates math and reading into other subjects such as history, science, and the arts. Based on the Reading Counts concept, Math Counts is a Synergy-created competition that begins in December and ends in January. Teachers teach a combination of grade-level and foundational-level math skills, so that by December students should have mastered key math skills that have been identified as essential for that grade level.

Starting in December every grade level has a packet of tests for the students, and they may take the tests as many times as they need to in order to pass. The tests comprise twenty-five to fifty basic number-sense problems (timed and untimed). Students who pass their tests receive a medal at a ceremony at the end of January. This strategy has reaped great benefits for Synergy students as the percentage of students receiving medals equates to the percentage of proficient and advanced students on the CSTs. The first year Math Counts was implemented, 75 percent of the students received medals, and 78 percent were proficient and advanced on the CST. Last year, 90 percent received medals, and nearly 93 percent were proficient and advanced.

A major component of Synergy's success is ensuring that all staff share the same philosophy of learning. As Synergy's Creed states, "At Synergy, we're all in this together because together we are better. We bring out the best in each other and in ourselves, every day in every way."

A rigorous hiring process carefully screens applicants. The first step for candidates is to respond to several essay questions. As an example, one of the questions will be about teaching style. Ms. Epps elaborates, "There are many great teaching styles—constructivism, project-based learning—these are not bad, but they're not what we do. We are all about the direct instruction model. So if that's what you want, it's not a good fit."

Another question might ask why so many schools in the inner city are failing. If the candidate writes a litany of blame on all external factors (parents, poverty, lack of English, etc.), again there is not a fit. If Ms. Epps is satisfied with the answers to all of the questions, the candidate is invited in to attend an informational meeting to hear about the Synergy vision. Then Synergy teachers are invited in to ask the candidate any questions they choose. If the candidate passes this part of the hiring protocol, a demonstration lesson is the next step, and finally an interview. Synergy Academies is the first charter school organization in Los Angeles to implement an intentional collaborative colocation strategy. Synergy Charter Academy shares a campus with a traditional district school, Quincy Jones Elementary School, but this partnership is more than two schools physically located in the same facility.

The Palisocs believe that there must be replicability in what they are doing. Ms. Epps concurs: "It cannot be that going to a Synergy school in the inner city is the only way to get a good education. We want to change the community—not just three hundred kids." The two schools share classroom space as well as the auditorium, library, and playground space. Both operate on the same bell schedule with 180 days of school. Students from both schools are on the yard together at 7:52 a.m. for the Pledge of Allegiance and announcements and are in the classrooms at 8:00 a.m. sharp to start instruction.

There is a positive reciprocal relationship between the administrators of both schools. Mr. Palisoc presented professional development to both schools' staffs about the Synergy Power Over Words and Power Over Numbers strategies. Other than the fact that Quincy's uniform shirts are green and Synergy's are maroon, it is difficult to separate the two schools.

A concrete example of the collaborative nature of the two schools is the way recess is structured. When Synergy first opened its school in 2004, it began with a free-play recess, and it immediately found it to be too chaotic. Students did not return to class calm and focused enough for instruction, and too much time was lost. A change was made the next day. Now the entire yard is organized in zones.

Synergy brought this best practice to its collaborative campus so that both schools now have organized recess at the same time. The students are separated by grade level with each grade level wearing a different colored pinny. Students are then assigned to the different zones where they exercise and are taught specific skills and games. This highly structured program has markedly reduced discipline problems and improved the teachers' ability to engage students in learning without wasting precious instructional minutes.

Especially noteworthy are Synergy's Scholar Lessons. These are a variety of citizenship and life-skills lessons that were created by Mr. Palisoc to help students when they were struggling academically or behaviorally. As Ms. Epps shares, "These were Randyisms for the longest time. Then we typed them all up and everyone uses them." They are posted in every classroom in both Synergy and Quincy Jones with both schools' names on them. They are introduced in the morning very quickly, once a day, and then reinforced by the teachers all year.

#1 EYE Contact = BRAIN Contact
#2 Do it RIGHT or do it AGAIN
#3 When there is teacher talk, there is no student talk.
#4 Don't make up your own procedures.
#5 We make requests, not demands.
#6 Don't ignore. Respond.
#7 Do the RIGHT thing. When no one is looking, do the right thing ANYWAY.

#8   Everything comes with a cost. Consider the cost of your actions.
#9   Recognize the problem. Don't become the problem.
#10 Bring out the best in each other.
#11 Don't read to finish. <u>Read to understand.</u>
#12 Self-monitor.
#13 Don't PICK your answer. DEFEND your answer.
#14 Explain.
#15 Don't do as little as you can, do as best as you can.
#16 The way you practice is the way you perform.
#17 Conduct yourselves as ladies and gentlemen.
#18 When you win, do not brag. When you lose, do not show anger.
#19 Everybody has common sense. Not everybody uses it. Students here will use common sense.
#20 We sit and stand like scholars.

In addition to sitting and standing like scholars, students walk with their hands behind their backs when they walk. The belief is that it helps get the students focused and ready to learn, and keeps their hands off each other and the walls. Raul and Armida Barrera are parents of nine children, two of whom attended Synergy Charter Academy. One is now at Synergy Kinetic Academy middle school, and the other at Synergy Quantum Academy high school. They are happy with the strict discipline policy at all three schools. "We like discipline. Children need that. It is a change for the kids. You have to follow rules; you have to be respectful to other people. They provide that for my kids and you can see the difference."

The Barreras are pleased with how parents have been included in their children's education. Synergy encourages both mothers and fathers to attend meetings and trainings, which are held at times when working parents can attend—evenings and Saturdays. As Ms. Epps adds, "There's a lot of blame put on lack of parent involvement—well, have you educated them? Have you held a meeting at night? On the weekend? Have you stood outside the day of or before the meeting as the principal, talking to every parent as they're dropping off their kids, handing out a flyer saying 'hope to see you tonight?' What have you really done to try to educate these parents? Anyone can hold a meeting at 8:00 in the morning."

A parent survey identifies what training the parents would like to have next year. Mrs. Barrera adds, "They tell you what the students are learning each semester so you can check their homework. They tell you how you can help them. Every day you check and sign your child's homework. And read—we have to listen to them even if you don't speak English."

FUTURE PLANS

Cognizant of the charter school law's mandate to be "incubators of best practices," the Palisocs are committed to sharing Synergy's best practices. As Meg Palisoc puts it, "We never opened charter schools to be antidistrict or political. All schools should be like this. It shouldn't matter whether you're at a Synergy school or at a charter school. This is what American public schools should be like for everybody, regardless of your background, income, inner city, urban, suburban. What's best for one is best for all—that's what our belief is."

In the 2011/2012 school year Synergy Trade Secrets Tours were implemented. They are so named because so many people had said, "Your scores are amazing, what are your secrets?" These two-hour events include presentations on the history and mission of the school and successful practices that have closed the achievement gap for their students. After this information is shared, the participants are invited to tour the school, visit classrooms, and see the teachers in action. After the tour, there is a question-and-answer session with Ms. Palisoc, Ms. Epps, and a group of student leaders.

During the first year of implementation, four tours were held. The goal is to hold one of these sessions a month and continue this practice with Synergy Kinetic Academy and Synergy Quantum Academy. The Palisocs are exploring ways to share their "secrets" on a greater scale. Opening a Professional Development Center where school teams could come to learn, and sending a Synergy team out to schools to observe and assist in their improvement, are options being explored.

CONCLUSIONS

When asked if they had been willing to lose their house if their vision didn't work, Meg Palisoc answered, "Yes, it's worth it to us to sacrifice—for the chance and opportunity to do something big that we believed we could do . . . to try to start a school, work with kids in a tough neighborhood and transform it. So we're pretty excited about what we've been able to do."

The Palisocs have reason to be proud. In addition to being the highest-performing kindergarten through grade five school in South Los Angeles (2006, 2007, 2008, 2009, 2010, 2011), a partial list of their accomplishments includes:

2007	Charter School Excellence Award
	ExEd–Siart Foundation
2007	National Charter School of the Year
	Center for Education Reform
2008	California Distinguished School
	California Department of Education
2008	California Charter School of the Year
	California Charter Schools Association
2008/2009	Title I Academic Achievement Award
	California Department of Education
	National Blue Ribbon Award
	United States Department of Education
2013	Gold Winner—Best Urban Elementary School in America
	National Center for Urban School Transformation

Mrs. Barrera sums it up. "I feel so privileged to be part of what they're doing. I'm so sorry that my other seven kids didn't get to have this." Students at Synergy Charter Academy are flourishing in a very disciplined, structured environment. But, as Ms. Epps puts it, "We have a ton of fun." This comment was made as she raced out to participate in Water Day.

Water Day is an annual celebration for students who had perfect attendance during the two weeks of testing (whether they are in tested grades or not). The students get to throw balls soaked with water at each other and teachers for twenty minutes. Never losing sight of the urgency of their quest for educational equity in the inner city, "fun" activities reward the students' hard work and commitment to their own improvement both academically and socially.

KEY ELEMENTS

- The core curriculum is supplemented by innovative curricula such as Power Over Words, Power Over Numbers, Reading Counts, and Step Up To Writing.
- There is a rigorous hiring process that ensures that incoming teachers fully embrace the Synergy philosophy and will be successful using the Synergy methods.
- The Scholar Lessons are used consistently by all staff to teach students important citizenship and life-skills lessons.

Part II

CHARTER MIDDLE SCHOOLS

CHAPTER 5

Lakeview Charter Academy
Lake View Terrace, California

INTRODUCTION

Partnerships to Uplift Communities (PUC) schools was founded as a result of two visionary leaders meeting and discovering that they had a common mission to improve secondary students' achievement in densely populated urban areas plagued by low student achievement and high dropout rates. Dr. Jacqueline Elliot and Dr. Ref Rodriguez met in 1998 after independently receiving charter school planning grants from the California Department of Education. Dr. Elliot was focused primarily on making a change for the students in the northeast San Fernando Valley, while Dr. Rodriquez held the same concerns for the students in Northeast Los Angeles.

In 1999 Dr. Rodriguez supported Dr. Elliot as she developed and opened Community Charter Middle School, the first charter middle school in Los Angeles. Dr. Rodriguez, with Dr. Elliot's help, opened the California Academy for Liberal Studies Middle School (CALS) in the fall of 2000. Immediately, these two highly successful schools had extensive waiting lists and an outcry from the community for more seats.

Responding to this need, two more schools were opened—a high school for CALS graduates (CALS Early College High School) in 2003, and Lakeview Charter Academy in 2004. Believing that a cluster of charter schools in a community reaped benefits for students and the community, Drs. Elliot and Rodriguez founded the PUC charter school development and management corporation.

Since then, PUC has opened ten new middle and high schools, including the Lakeview Charter High School in 2010, bringing the total number of PUC schools to thirteen. Schools are added slowly to make sure that the right leadership and teachers are in place, so generally there are no dips in test scores. Schools are opened with one grade level, to provide consistency and inculcation into the PUC culture. Part of the vision of PUC schools is to open its doors to any and all students from an elementary school.

A new LAUSD requirement mandates that any students who live in Lake View Terrace will be accepted without participating in a lottery. This mandate fits well with Lakeview's mission of wanting to be an integral part of the community—trying to "uplift the community."

Lakeview began in 2004 in an office park building with only enough space for sixth grade. That class looped for three years at that location until the PUC Valley Educational Complex was developed by the Pacific Charter School Development Corporation, where it moved to in 2008.

Lakeview shares the property with Community Charter Middle School, and Community Charter Early College High School; the three schools share the multipurpose room and performance space. As the principal, Dr. Manuel Ponce Jr., shares, "It's a lesson in collaboration." The school is at its student capacity of 340 with a waiting list of 200 for sixth grade and 100 each for the seventh and eighth grades.

The ethnic breakdown of Lakeview's 345 students is 1 percent White, 1 percent Asian/Filipino/Pacific Islander, 95 percent Hispanic, and 1 percent African American. Approximately 90 percent of the students are on the Free and Reduced-Price Lunch Program (Socioeconomically Disadvantaged), 13 percent are ELs, and 13 percent are SWDs. Lakeview's API rose from 708 in 2005/2006 to 843 in 2012/2013. The school met thirteen of thirteen AYP indicators and remains free of Program Improvement sanctions.

Lakeview is clearly a data-driven school. Data Director and Zoom Data are utilized to pinpoint students' strengths and weaknesses on specific standards. The principal requires that teachers review areas of weakness and revisit their lesson plans to identify what needs to be changed the next time those standards are taught. Teachers participate in four days of professional development before the school year begins

Data Implications

Year	Enrollment	Ethnicity				
		% AI	% Asian/Filipino/ Pacific Islander	% Black	% Hispanic	% White
2012–13	345	0.6	1.4	1.2	95.1	0.6
2011–12	347	0.3	1.2	2.9	95.1	0.6
2010–11	313	0.3	1.6	5.1	91.7	1.3

Year	% Socioeconomic	% English Learners	% Students w/ Disabilities
2012–13	90.1	12.8	12.9
2011–12	88.8	13.8	12.9
2010–11	92.3	15.3	11.6

Year	API	% AYP—English Lang Arts*	% Mathematics*
2012–13	843	58.5	66.6
2011–12	856	64.5	73.6
2010–11	867	63.5	77.9

* = Percent at/above Proficient

to analyze data and to project what their instruction will look like in the classroom in the upcoming year.

In addition, four benchmark assessments are given throughout the year. One full day of professional development is held in December after the first benchmark, a full day in March after the second benchmark, and one day at the end of the year—all focused on data analysis and using those data to make instructional decisions. Teachers turn in their lesson plans for the week every Monday morning. The principal provides feedback more in the form of inquiry (with newer teachers receiving more help). Questions are asked such as, "What were the learning experiences like? Was it too much direct instruction? Did you have graphic organizers? Did you just do PowerPoints?"

There are no department chairs. All teachers can be teacher leaders. There is a professional development (PD) team, which puts together a PD scope and sequence for the whole year. They plan the PDs and make presentations. It is a collaborative effort, with the team meeting weekly. Dr. Ponce believes in "teachers leading teachers and giving them everything they need, the support they need, and then getting out of their way."

Intervention is held after school for any students who require it. Teachers create lists of ten to fifteen students based on specific standards and place them in intervention classes that run in a cycle of four to five weeks. Pre-, mid-, and post-assessments are given.

When students test out, new students are placed in the classes. Each content area's intervention is held on a different day, enabling the student to take advantage of more than one intervention class. In addition, the English language arts teachers do additional Saturday school twice a month. Students may also benefit from tutoring assistance. Teachers have tutoring hours, which are part of the regular day. Many teachers are available before and after school and during nutrition and lunch.

Students are included in the data discussions. Teachers share information about CST and benchmark assessment data with the students so that they know what they need to do to improve. Students articulate, "I want to be advanced." "My goal is to be proficient." They are expected to track their own progress and set goals for their CSTs.

SUCCESS FACTORS

Lakeview adheres to the same three design principles followed in all PUC schools. The first design area (academics) provides an untracked academic program that prepares every student for college work, beginning in sixth grade. Originally students were in classes of twenty-five, but because of budget cuts, the classes have risen to twenty-nine or thirty. There is a longer school day; school begins at 7:40 a.m. and ends at 3:10 p.m. The extended-day program begins after school and ends at 6:00 p.m. This program includes tutoring, clubs, activities, homework club, science, yearbook, cooking, theater, and music. Athletic programs, which include flag football, volleyball, basketball, soccer, and cheerleading, are offered.

At Lakeview all students are considered gifted and taught to those rigorous standards. Teachers have had extensive training in the California Association for the Gifted teaching strategies proposed by Dr. Sandra Kaplan of the University of Southern California (USC). Depth and complexity icons are posted and utilized in all classrooms. As teacher Vartan Shohmelian tells it, "We treat all students as if they're gifted. That's what we believe. It speeds up student learning because we purposefully design our lessons that way—it really accelerates their learning."

In the sixth grade, Lakeview has a unique system for filling in the deficits those students bring when coming from elementary. All sixth-grade students participate in a Learning Lab once a week. All core teachers teach their classes four times a week. On the fifth day, the students attend the Learning Lab (with their teacher). The students are given a computer-based diagnostic at the beginning of the year, so that during Learning Lab the students are put to work on the computers using data-driven programs such as Study Island and Teen Biz to work on specific standards. While the class is engaged in individualized intervention, the teacher pulls small groups of students together to differentiate instruction for those who need it.

Most special-education students are fully included in the general education classes. There are two full-time inclusion specialists who push into class and pull students out. Inclusion specialists co-plan and co-teach with the general education teachers, and provide professional development for them to ensure that teachers are equipped to meet their students' needs. In addition, there is a Scholar Success Center (Learning Center) utilized for students with moderate to severe learning disabilities. Depending on their Individualized Education Program (IEP) goals, students go to the Scholar Success Center to receive one-on-one assistance in English and mathematics.

English learners (ELs) are also fully included. Mr. Shohmelian elaborates, "We believe they need to interact with students with proficient levels of English. We believe in academic discourse that creates a culture where students are not humiliated if they share ideas and thoughts and feelings. The students teach each other. It gets them speaking at high levels. It gets them ready so that when they walk into that college class, nothing catches them by surprise." The computer program Teen Biz has proved effective in supporting ELs in the Learning Lab.

At Lakeview, as at all PUC schools, the arts are considered core, and fundamental to student success. The belief is that when students do well in the arts, they do better in their academic subjects. Dr. Ponce clarifies, "We have students who need to find their niche, and art could be what keeps them in school, just like sports for some kids. They find what really speaks to them." In sixth grade, students receive nine weeks of visual arts, music (African drumming), dance, theater, speech, and debate.

In seventh grade, they have a semester of dance and a semester of theater. In eighth grade, they have a semester of theater and a semester of visual arts. The goal is to provide a sample of everything so that by the time they get to high school, they can take what they love and be more motivated. Besides learning new skills and discipline-specific language, students improve in creative problem solving, time management, self-esteem, and critical-thinking skills. Students also participate in regular physical education classes that provide them with a variety of experiences so that they have an idea of what interests them when they get to high school.

The second design area shared by all PUC schools is school culture—a school culture that won't allow any student to fail. An exciting program for incoming sixth graders is their immersion in college culture before beginning at Lakeview. For a week in the summer preceding sixth grade, students are bused to California State University Northridge (CSUN). They are taught a series of scholar lessons. For example, students will read about a scientist and discuss what made that person a scholar—what enabled him to get where he was (perseverance, for example).

Students will have lessons on routines and procedures (how they enter and leave class, how they ask questions, how they speak to each other) to ingrain them in the culture of the school. It isn't all work; students get to eat in the university food court and swim in the pool for PE one day. At the end of eighth grade, the students return to CSUN to walk the stage and culminate.

Collaboration is the norm at Lakeview. Teachers come together to talk about best practices so that when students go from class to class, there is consistency in the strategies used to meet certain needs. For example, teachers will come together as teams to talk about a practice that would improve students' ability to speak like scholars. This practice is then taught and reinforced in every class.

Not only is there consistency in academics, there is consistency in expectations for behavioral norms. Students wear uniforms and are expected to tuck in their shirts. Talking out and disrespect are not permitted. All students must answer in complete sentences and explain their thinking. They must use the language of the discipline and appropriate vocabulary words. Everyone is responsible for every student. As teacher Mandy Gibbs elaborates, "There's no secret sauce—there's no one thing. Consistency is a big thing. That's what makes the difference between good results and amazing results."

All students are required to demonstrate their commitment to their community by providing community service. In order to go to grad night, students must perform thirty-five hours of community service. Students with more than sixty hours receive special recognition during graduation ceremonies. Also, students participate in clean-up crews that go into the neighborhood; they wear PUC vests and beautify their surroundings. The seventh grade goes to the beach at the end of the year for a beach cleanup.

The third design area relates to organizational practices that are common to all PUC schools. Every PUC school has the same learning cycle for all teachers. It includes an opening that is tailored to the content (called a "Do Now"); this time could also include checking and collecting homework or a quick skill review. Then the lesson includes accessing prior knowledge (APK), extending prior knowledge (EPK), application, and reflection with an exit ticket.

Students know the learning cycle very well and can articulate where they are, and are supposed to be, in any lesson. They know what to expect when they're coming into class, they know how to ask questions, and they know what dimensions of depth and complexity help them to work through their content. Therefore teachers can start at a higher level because time is not wasted reteaching routines and procedures.

Teachers do not have pacing plans or textbooks they must follow. Dr. Ponce clarifies, "Teachers are the architects of their own curriculum. They put together, based on what they know, their expertise, and their data, what needs to be taught first and why—what needs to be next. And then they collaborate with the grade level above them—what do I need to emphasize more? Driven by data in their class. . . . it doesn't matter to me if they use a book, teacher-created materials, a YouTube clip, movie—whatever it takes to get the students to engage, discover, and understand that material—it's up to the teacher."

A consortium of charter school organizations received a Gates grant for teacher evaluation. The consortium included Green Dot, Alliance, and Aspire, and the Teacher Effectiveness Framework has been tailored by PUC to reflect constructivism and college readiness. This framework includes all aspects of teaching (classroom environment, lesson planning, instruction, professionalism, collaboration, and how teachers are evaluated). Although technically an evaluation system, Dr. Ponce describes it as a teacher-development system in place to build capacity.

The system is based around growth goals. The first step in developing these growth goals is collaboration between the teacher and principal to examine evidence to select three goals for the year. Because the evidence compellingly demonstrated a school-wide need, academic discourse became one of the goals for every teacher. Teachers who have the same growth goal come together in PODs (peer-organized development teams) to observe each other, give each other feedback, plan together, and collaborate to help each other to get better on the growth goal.

Teachers rate themselves individually, and the principal rates them. They bring artifacts and come together with the principal to discuss what is occurring in the teacher's practice. The process includes both informal and formal observations. To support the teachers further, there is a dashboard on the Internet where there are videos and articles relating to the growth-goal topics. Teachers are expected to own their own growth with the support and guidance of the administrators.

PUC has adopted a hiring protocol across all their schools, but Lakeview was permitted to modify it slightly. Dr. Ponce calls the prospective teacher to meet with him first before going on to anything else. The interview is one-on-one in order to give the teacher an accurate picture of the school and expectations. The next step is an interview panel with three or four teachers and several candidates. Questions are asked about philosophy such as, "How do you support your students? What would you do if half of your class is struggling?" The candidates are given the task of creating a professional development for a first-year teacher. They are given twenty minutes to work collaboratively on the task while the panel fishbowls the process.

The ideal candidates are reflective practitioners who are open to feedback and open to talking with other teachers about their practice.

Candidates who make it to the next step teach a demonstration lesson and are given feedback. How well feedback is received is noted. The students who participated in the demonstration lesson are given a survey to share their perspective on the negatives and positives of the lesson. The final decision for hiring is made by the panel. For every open position, the panel may see twenty to thirty candidates. This extensive process is in place to ensure that the person selected is a good fit for the culture of the school.

There is a mentoring program at PUC. Every adult at PUC has two or three college students (former PUC students) to support. The adults e-mail and call them to maintain that connection to the community. It is a tangible reminder that the PUC family continues to support them.

FUTURE PLANS

PUC schools were opened based on data that said that another middle or high school was needed. Always paramount was the question: Do we have enough families committed to being part of our schools and sharing our vision? In the immediate future, no new schools are planned. As Dr. Ponce reminds, "There may be one or two more schools, but we feel that we're really where we want and need to be. It is getting harder to get things approved, and harder to get space. If the demand in the community is there, and everything falls into place, we are always open to the opportunity."

CONCLUSIONS

PUC schools have three commitments: (1) five times more college graduates within the communities we serve; (2) after four years with us, students will be proficient; and (3) we commit to uplift our communities now and forever. Lakeview Charter Academy clearly has demonstrated dedication to these commitments as it continues to provide a rigorous college-preparatory curriculum and the scaffolding supports to ensure that every student succeeds at the highest levels.

KEY ELEMENTS

- Lakeview Charter Academy is a data-driven school. Data Director and Zoom Data support in-depth analysis and planning by the principal, teachers, and students.
- Academic support is provided through four- to five-week intervention programs based on specific student deficits.
- Sixth-grade students attend a Learning Lab to address areas of concern identified in an entrance assessment.
- The Teacher Effectiveness Framework serves as a teacher-evaluation and teacher-development system.
- Consistent use of the lesson cycle, icons of depth and complexity, and procedures ensures that valuable time is not wasted. As students move from class to class and grade to grade, they know exactly what the expectations are for them.

CHAPTER 6

Valor Academy Middle School
Arleta, California

INTRODUCTION

Founder and head of school Hrag Hamalian's personal experience served as the impetus and inspiration for Valor Academy Middle School. Born of Lebanese Armenian parents, Mr. Hamalian came to the United States when he was two years old and started school as a second-language learner. After graduation from Boston College, his passion for education was realized when he became a Teach for America teacher and was assigned as a ninth-grade biology teacher at Locke High School in Watts (part of the Los Angeles Unified School District).

The abysmal graduation rate and even worse rate of graduates matriculating to college were eye opening. He was struck by the dichotomy of their disparate lives. As he put it, "I had a great public education, was an immigrant, and I was watching kids with the same characteristics fail—this is ridiculous! It was insane for me to be teaching high school kids going on fifteen, sixteen years of age who couldn't read and thought they were going to college."

Hamalian availed himself of leadership opportunities at Locke. He became the department chair. With a group of like-minded teachers, he formulated a small school and within days saw a difference could be made by holding students accountable for even simple things like turning in homework and attendance. It made him see the possibilities—if he could accomplish this much at Locke High School, what could be accomplished if he started a school from scratch? At the age of twenty-two, he determined to do just that.

Hamalian enrolled in the Building Excellent Schools program, which trains entrepreneurs to open high-performing charter schools in urban communities. He spent a year visiting high-performing charters to observe best practices, and spent a year planning as a resident at a KIPP (Knowledge is Power Program) school. He then looked for a location where a charter school would be welcomed and embraced. He believed that it was important to demonstrate the importance to a community of a charter. It was important to ensure that the community really felt a part of the school.

After a year of building relationships with the community by visiting neighborhood councils, churches, Rotary Clubs, etc., Hamalian found that the North Hollywood/Panorama City/Arleta community was very open to having a charter. Since it was a primarily Spanish bilingual community, he spent time building alliances with people in the community who could advocate for the school on his behalf. Martha Killbourn was such an advocate. She was unhappy with the educational experience of her fourth-grade daughter who was attending a local LAUSD school.

After attending a local neighborhood council meeting where Mr. Hamalian was asking permission to start a charter school, she asked what she could do to help. She helped to spread the word in the community, and when Mr. Hamalian asked her to enroll her daughter at Valor, she agreed. She proudly says, "My daughter was the first student for the whole school where there were no classrooms, no teachers, no building, nothing—just the dream and desire of Mr. Hamalian."

Valor Academy Middle School opened its doors in 2009 with a class of fifth graders in a rented fifty-year-old church. One grade was added each year, and in the 2012/2013 school year, the school added the eighth grade. Currently, there are 472 students in grades five through eight in four classes of thirty or thirty-one students at each grade. Students in each grade proudly wear uniforms that signify their grade (fifth–maroon, sixth–gray, seventh–navy, and eighth–shirt and tie). Ninety-nine percent of the students come from within a five-mile radius; the remaining 1 percent comes from a ten-mile radius. All grade-level eligible pupils are invited to attend Valor Academy. If the amount who apply exceeds the capacity (120 per grade level), a lottery

Data Implications

Year	Enrollment	% AI	% Asian/Filipino/ Pacific Islander	% Black	% Hispanic	% White
			Ethnicity			
2012–13	472	0	3.4	2.3	88.1	4.7
2011–12	317	0	4.4	4.7	83.3	7.3
2010–11	235	0	5.1	6.8	80.4	7.7

Year	% Socioeconomic	% English Learners	% Students w/ Disabilities
2012–13	89.0	15.2	11.9
2011–12	93.4	13.8	10.4
2010–11	93.0	34.7	7.9

Year	API	% AYP—English Lang Arts*	% Mathematics*
2012–13	880	66.7	81.8
2011–12	888	66.5	86.2
2010–11	850	55.7	75.4

* = Percent at/above Proficient

is held. Preference for admission is given to students who reside in the LAUSD, and to siblings of current students.

An eighth-grade class was added to Valor in the 2012/2013 school year, bringing the current enrollment to 472 students. The ethnic breakdown is 5 percent White, 3 percent Asian/Filipino/Pacific Islander, 88 percent Hispanic, and 2 percent African American. Approximately 89 percent of the students are on the Free and Reduced-Price Lunch Program (Socioeconomically Disadvantaged), 15 percent are ELs, and 12 percent are SWDs.

In the 2009/2010 school year, Valor's API for fifth grade was 835. In the 2011/2012 school year, it rose to 888 for grades five through seven and won the California Distinguished School Award. In 2012/2013 all grades had an API of 880. The school met thirteen of seventeen AYP indicators, failing to meet proficiency levels in English Language Arts (ELA) for its African American, Hispanic, Socioeconomically Disadvantaged, and EL populations.

For three weeks during the summer, staff comes together to review STAR (standardized testing and reporting) data so that students' strengths and weaknesses in relation to the standards can be mapped.

These data are used for teachers to create their unit plans and scope and sequences that are turned into the director of instruction before school begins. Midterms and finals are given every six weeks to benchmark student progress, which determines whether students have improved, stayed the same, or declined by level.

Teachers are required to write a differentiated action plan (DAP) for their students, which are also turned into the director of instruction. The entire school reviews and discusses the results of the DAPs to determine support. For example, if there has been a decline in ELA, the math team looks for ways to support ELA development by using the same academic language in their classes and/or aligning their objectives with those of the ELA teachers. In addition to the three weeks to prepare for the school year, teachers collaborate during professional development on Fridays and six pupil-free days. This is done to track students' progress to ensure that the right instruction is being delivered to every student.

After-school mandatory tutoring is provided during the year for students who are struggling. Tutoring classes are small with no more than fifteen students per class, and are grade-level/subject specific. Parents are informed that the students are required to attend. Each teacher is responsible for providing tutoring once a week.

SUCCESS FACTORS

Although most schools have a "college-going culture," Valor has created an environment that inculcates students into the university system from day one. Mr. Hamalian selected premiere local universities that have become partners in Valor's mission to ensure that students know that college is in their future.

When students enter Valor in the fifth grade, they are placed in one of four universities (UCLA, USC, Loyola Marymount, or Pepperdine). So, at each grade level, there is a class of thirty in each of the four universities. Students in fifth and sixth grade stay in their university (homeroom/advisory) throughout the day. In seventh and eighth grade, students meet in their university, then are mixed up socially (not by level) for classes, and return to their university at the end of the day.

They maintain their university identities for all four years, and graduate as a "UCLA Scholar," or "Pepperdine Scholar," etc.

During their four years at Valor, students will visit all four universities. In fifth grade they visit their own university. In sixth grade they visit their rival university, and in seventh and eighth grade they will visit the other two universities. During this time, university students and alumni come out to speak to and mentor students. A very tangible link is forged with students building a desire to go to college.

To further build pride in their universities, three times a year students participate in a cheer fest. School is stopped at 2:00 p.m. and schools are paired off (e.g., UCLA v. USC). Students and teachers plan for weeks developing fight songs, chants, and costumes (across all four grade levels). The connection to the university is so strong that if you ask students if they're going to college, everyone will say "Yes." Martha Killbourn shared that her daughter's bedroom is blue and yellow. "She's dreaming to go to UCLA."

There is a strong focus on preparing students for high school and beyond. According to director of instruction Jessica Boro, "Ultimately our goal is to ensure that our students leave us in eighth grade with a strong background in mathematics, having passed algebra before going into high school. For ELA, we want our students to leave reaching fluency and prepared to write any entrance exam for the top-performing high schools and later on for colleges." To achieve these goals, students in fifth and sixth grades have a double block of ELA (one hour of reading and one hour of writing) each day. In mathematics, they receive one hour of number sense and one hour of problem solving each day.

In seventh and eighth grades the students have one period of math and one period of ELA, however the periods are longer (seventy-five minutes). In addition, students have access to the standards-based computer program Study Island. This allows students to have extra practice in ELA and math at their own levels.

Instructional aides also support students by either team teaching or pulling small groups of students for extra support. Teachers' lesson plans, PowerPoints, and digital notes are all stored on the school's server so that the aides have access to the tools that ensure coherence to what the teachers are doing in the classroom.

The extended time in math and ELA does not preclude students from taking other core subjects. Students attend school from 8:00 a.m. to 3:45 p.m. on Monday, Tuesday, Wednesday, and Thursday. On Friday students are dismissed at 2:30 p.m. to allow for professional development. Free academic supports and tutoring are available to all students until 5:00 p.m. every day. In addition, all students have thirty minutes of practice per night for all of their core subjects.

More time for instruction is saved by the consistency in the structures at Valor. In fifth and sixth grade, students stay in their university (homeroom) the entire day, and their different teachers rotate into the classroom. In fifth and sixth grade, all classes look the same. Systems are very structured, down to the binders the students have, the notebooks that they're expected to keep, and the way they organize them. Procedures are in place for how students line up, how they move their tables for groups, and how they hand off the computers to the next class. The first two years build up the organizational structure so that when the students reach seventh grade, they change classes quickly, quietly, and peacefully.

A great deal of meticulous work and planning went into the development of these structures. Mr. Hamalian shares that he spent two years thinking about how to build a good culture at a school by looking at other models and bringing in best practices. First-year teacher Taryn Song appreciated the structures in place. "As a first-year teacher, I tell people it is challenging, but I couldn't have been in a better place because of the support I have from my colleagues and administration, and the systems already in place. I believe in the systems. It made my first-year experience positive."

A strong component of the school culture is the PREP model. PREP stands for Prepared, Respectful, Engaged, and Professional. At the end of every class, every day, the teachers and the students have a one- to two-minute discussion about how well they were PREPed. For Prepared, points are given for having completed all of the homework and having the necessary materials. For Respect, was there any interrupting or eye rolling? If so, points are lost. Classes compete with the other classes on their grade level. The class with the highest points wins the honor of displaying their grade level's prize (Leo the Lion for fifth, a rain stick for sixth, etc.).

The PREP system also applies for individual students. Students earn merits and demerits based on the same four core values. Students receive a weekly report (paycheck) that lets them know how many PREP points they have to use to make purchases. Students can participate in a monthly auction to bid on donated Lakers or Dodger tickets. Or they can bid on having lunch with a teacher, or being the principal for a day. Teacher Nathan Karisu's wife baked cookies, and they went to the highest bid of ten thousand points! Founding teacher Angie Tree points out, "There is a lot of consistency. It is such a solid system that has really supported me to be free to teach how I want to teach because I have such a solid system to support me."

Contributing to the culture are yearly home visits. After the second trimester, each teacher makes a visit to each student's home to build the community and bridge the gap between home and school. The focus of these visits is not academic (that is handled in conferences). Rather, this is a time to learn more about the student's family on a personal level. Teacher Taryn Song finds the visits enlightening. "It's awesome to see their homes and where they come from. A lot of times we share a meal with them. The students are interested to see that teachers have a life outside of school and we have our own families and hobbies."

There are many opportunities for character development. For example, life-skills classes are taught by Mr. Hamalian and Ms. Boro in the fifth and sixth grades. Every Friday there is a Community Circle. Every other week the grade levels have the opportunity to hold their own assembly when they review items important to their grade level. The PREP values and the students' progress on meeting those values are reviewed. Council is held once a week and provides ways for students to share out and resolve issues in their lives.

The high expectations for behavior have created a student body that is respectful. This is nowhere more evident than in the Student Ambassador program. Students who exhibit exemplary behavior and are models of the PREP values are selected to represent the school at functions and serve as leaders among the students. All students are taught proper social etiquette as part of professionalism. They are taught to be professional whether dealing with an adult or a peer. This is taught and modeled from day one of fifth grade, and the language is used constantly.

"This is the professional way to respond. This is the professional way to approach someone."

Every few months Valor holds a community breakfast to which are invited community members, neighborhood council members, university liaisons, and as Mr. Hamalian says, "Anyone and everyone who will come to the school." The purpose is for them to come to the school and be brought up to date on what is happening. It is a way to continually forge partnerships with the community and to ensure that the community sees Valor as their school. At this function, the student ambassadors greet the guests with a handshake, and proudly escort them on a tour of classrooms. The students are poised and articulate and professional.

FUTURE PLANS

Mr. Hamalian is currently pursuing his MBA. He believes that part of the school's success can be attributed to the fact that he runs it like a business and wants to make sure that Valor is part of what's going to be an expanding organization; that he's leading it in a way that ensures that it grows in a positive way.

He wants to guard against the problem of "taking one successful model and then building out five more and then the academic quality of all of them declines." He further states, "In future years, many years down the line, if we felt we had mastered the middle school model, and we had an organization that was sustainable, and we'd become a premiere source of what it means to be a charter middle school, at that point I would take the lead to try something new. But we're not there."

Very aware of the parents' need for good high school options, they have created a high school placement process that presents all of the public, charter, private, and parochial options that are open to them. There is a class for seventh-grade students called "High School Placement for Seventh Graders" that they take once a week. Information sessions have helped allay the parents' fears. Every student has applied to the LAUSD magnet schools. The Valor staff actually filled out the applications for them. In addition, since there are ten charter high schools surrounding Valor, every student was required to turn in a charter application.

Jessica Boro also pushes for a slow-growth model. "After we've been a middle school and graduated a couple of classes and know what works, then let's go on to do other things that would benefit the community. At the end of the day, it must be a benefit to the community. Valor should have an opportunity to stand in this community for decades to come if we do it right." But, she adds, "We deserve to have a home—somewhere where we can decorate it and plaster student work and have a parent room where we train our parents to work with their students at home and really meet the needs of the students."

Although committed to the slow-growth model in terms of opening more middle schools, the concern with the lack of high-performing high school slots and in order to ensure a smooth matriculation to high school for their eighth-grade students, Valor is opening a high school. Partnering with the Bright Star charter organization, the new high school, which was started in the 2013/2014 school year with a ninth-grade class, is housed on a floor of Panorama High School. Students will now have the opportunity to graduate from high schools as Valor Scholars—students truly PREPed for the future.

CONCLUSIONS

Valor Academy became a reality because of the dream of Hrag Hamalian. He envisioned a school that would fulfill the need of the underserved communities of North Hollywood, Panorama City, and Arleta. Three years later, Valor Academy has made amazing progress in educating students from economically challenged families and has created a true college-going culture by partnering with four premiere universities in the Los Angeles area. In the three years of its existence, Valor Academy has outperformed the average of all schools in the LAUSD by 114 points on the API, and outperformed the average of all schools in California by 60 points.

This success has been accomplished through a combination of a longer school day, extended instruction in ELA and math, after-school academic supports, and a strong school culture that promotes Preparedness, Respect, Engagement, and Professionalism. Students are expected to rise to the highest expectations and are fully supported academically and socially.

Jessica Boro attributes some of the success to transparent communication across the board. From the board to the staff to families and the community at large, everyone is on the same page. Systems are in place so that expectations are known and embraced by all. Teachers are supported because "passionate educators create positive results for children. So if we don't stifle that creativity and that passion, then we're really going to create a movement that is going to be sustainable."

Hrag Hamalian was twenty-five years old when he founded Valor Academy. "I have been fortunate that at a young age people have seen something in me—I have leadership capability. We have a very successful school because people have entrusted me with moving things along in a positive way."

Martha Killbourn agrees. "It's like a diamond—something that shines—that's Valor Academy."

KEY ELEMENTS

- A true college-going culture exists for all students. Students understand the importance of higher education, know that they are supported, and are fully committed to attending college.
- Each teacher is required to examine their students' testing data and write a DAP for each student.
- A longer school day and specific supports are in place to ensure that all students succeed.

CHAPTER 7

View Park Preparatory Charter School
Los Angeles, California

INTRODUCTION

The corner of Crenshaw and Slauson is a crossroads common in South Los Angeles and other blighted urban areas around the country. Buses and cars run noisily north and south, east and west; vendors selling T-shirts populate each corner of the intersection where there are gas stations, fast food outlets, liquor stores, and churches. Amid the rush of people and vehicles sit stately brick buildings that house View Park Preparatory Charter Middle School and its adjacent high school.

This gated, quiet place of learning appears structured and focused, standing out in a neighborhood situated between the poverty of South Los Angeles and the affluence of nearby Windsor Hills, Ladera Heights, Marina Del Rey, and the bright beaches of the Pacific Ocean.

View Park Middle is one of thirteen schools managed by the Inner City Education Foundation (ICEF), all located in South Los Angeles and serving students from underperforming public schools. The community's demand for a quality educational program materialized into the creation of View Park Elementary School in 1999, a school with almost all low-income African American students. "At View Park we closed the achievement gap," founder Michael Piscal said. "On English tests, we scored as high as white students in suburban schools."

The ICEF College Readiness Model aims to create: (1) A College Going Culture; (2) College Study Habits; (3) Curriculum Backward Mapped from College Standards; (4) College Style Discourse; and (5) College Level Analytical Writing. ICEF schools work to achieve these goals through programs in athletics, performing and visual arts, and college counseling to enrich and support students' academic experience and help them define a path to college.

By 2005, with the help of Pacific Charter School Development, ICEF built the campus for the middle and high schools on the two-acre lot that had been vacant and blighted for over fifteen years. All ICEF schools use common textbooks and curriculum, in part so that students can transition smoothly from one ICEF school to another. The chief academic officer provides school directors with support in setting goals for students and staff, teacher evaluation and intervention, director coaching, and accessing best practices.

"The school was founded on the principle of the highest expectations. Everyone has a common core belief system they operated from, and those who come to the school share that vision," according to Kenya Jackson, director (principal). "The biggest challenge as director is wearing so many hats—discipline, impromptu parent meetings, teacher frustrations with the crises of life and work, being an instructional leader. You have to focus on results and be able to push your team to do their best."

The enrollment at View Park Middle is kept in the mid-three hundreds, and students are evenly dispersed in grades six through eight. "We retain most of our kids," according to Jackson. "It is hard to get a spot so most of them stay, but we do call people on our waiting list and invite them to enroll."

Ninety-five percent of View Park Middle's students are African American, 3 percent are Hispanic, 8 percent are SWDs, less than 1 percent are ELs, and 75 percent are Socioeconomically Disadvantaged. In the past View Park Middle had earned an API score of over 800 and was ranked seven or eight statewide and ten among similar schools. They had outperformed LAUSD schools consistently in all categories and bested statewide averages in the majority of areas.

However, the API has since slipped to 784, in part due to the performance of students with disabilities and the school's overall math scores. "Being here at the ICEF flagship school, and being 16 points away from that 800 API, I am very pressured—how do we get back to that magical number?" wonders Jackson. "The organization went through some bad financial times. Many teachers left and it became hard to attract people."

STAR test results show that the proficient and advanced percentages for English have remained above 50 percent, but math results fell to 45

Data Implications

Year	Enrollment	% AI	% Asian/Filipino/ Pacific Islander	% Black	% Hispanic	% White
			Ethnicity			
2012–13	344	0.3	0.6	95.3	2.9	0
2011–12	379	0	0	96.3	3.2	0.3
2010–11	342	0.6	0.6	96.2	2.0	0

Year	% Socioeconomic	% English Learners	% Students w/ Disabilities
2012–13	75.0	0.3	7.8
2011–12	62.5	0.5	6.3
2010–11	57.9	0	6.4

Year	API	% AYP—English Lang Arts*	% Mathematics*
2012–13	784	50.9	44.7
2011–12	774	50.5	40.1
2010–11	789	55.9	34.0

* = Percent at/above Proficient

percent in 2013. Using the data as a guide, Jackson is working with her math teachers on creating a new math curriculum to address the deficits the data show.

"Saxon Math is used across ICEF schools; but some teachers are using Glencoe online; Thurgood Marshall Middle has a blended learning model using Study Island and Revolution Prep; so they are doing something different," she says.

Students with disabilities scoring proficient and advanced in English remain at 12 percent and math rests at 8 percent. Due to the number of students with disabilities, the school is using its budget to fund more resource teachers and an aide and have implemented a co-teaching model for math and English. During study hall, these teachers work individually with students, and behavior/academic logs are used for students with or without IEPs in order to provide immediate intervention as needed.

The school has partnered with the California Science Center and the results have been remarkable. Students performed at 74 percent proficient/advanced on the 2013 science CSTs. "I love the active curriculum; it's amazing; our kids love science," Jackson said.

"In order to set our instructional goals for the year," states Jackson, "we look at data from the previous year to see where we fell short on our practices. We looked at questioning students and using various strategies in class." She runs data reports and looks at student grades at each marking period, which has resulted in a targeted professional-development session she presented on grading.

Jackson uses the school's data to focus her teachers and staff on providing appropriate interventions. The data created a Saturday school program from September to May that is flexible. Students are assigned to make up time if they were late during the week; others attend to get help to bolster slipping grades; for some students Saturday is a math and English workshop to help them fill in their learning gaps. This program is also used after school three days a week, giving students many opportunities, in addition to daily study hall, to meet the expectations of the school.

In addition to STAR testing, each department gives formative assessments every five weeks prior to the grading period. To support her staff, Jackson has presented professional development on how to write those assessments using state standards in order to get usable data to tailor instruction to meet the needs of all students.

SUCCESS FACTORS

Jackson identifies many factors that have contributed to the success of this school: parent support, excellent teachers and staff, active community organizations, and the school's organization. "The parents see that the mission of the school is realized," states Jackson. "We are considered a high-achieving charter school; our high school graduates 100 percent; 80 percent go to four-year universities with scholarships. The parents have bought into those results."

The school holds parent meetings every month and the mission and vision are reiterated through a code of excellence and choral response spoken at the end of every meeting. "We are in a process, we are not perfect, but we strive for excellence." At each meeting, cadres of parents break into grade-level groups and parents lead those sessions, discussing the calendar, fund-raising, student activities, and academic achievement.

Parents help raise money for their grade level and make decisions on how the money is spent. According to the student-parent handbook, parents are welcome to conduct impromptu and scheduled classroom observations. Parents also are required to attend orientation training to help them navigate the governance structure of the school and enhance their child's learning opportunities. Parents must volunteer a total of forty hours per family each school year, by helping with the after-school programs and attending meetings.

Jackson has used her experience as a teacher to provide a supportive yet demanding atmosphere for her teachers. "I preach consistency not perfection, academic passion, professionalism. It's modeled," she says. Jackson's leadership style fosters collaboration and teacher leadership, with teacher leaders guiding grade-level groups toward achieving school academic goals.

She also demands teachers reflect on their practice, always asking, "What can we do better?" She requires lesson plans each week for newer teachers and unit plans from veteran teachers, unless she sees something in her daily classroom observations that would warrant better evidence of planning. Teachers are observed formally twice a year. "It is a very thorough process, including a narrative account, teacher actions, student actions, best practices, and instructional goals," Jackson admits.

She uses a College Ready Promise-based formal evaluation process, modified by ICEF and driven by evidence to identify strengths and weaknesses to serve as a learning tool. Jackson is straightforward in her assessment of teachers and not afraid to push those she feels need pushing. She contacts her mentor, a more experienced principal, for assistance in dealing with challenging situations when teachers fail to meet expectations.

Additionally, Jackson has called in instructional coaches from ICEF to help her struggling teachers plan and manage their classrooms, but she will not sacrifice her students. All employees are hired "at will," and principals, after taking steps to mitigate any problems, will let go of teachers who do not meet the expectations of the school.

Along with standards-based curriculum, the teachers at View Park Middle have adopted school-wide teaching strategies including Socratic discourse, explicit vocabulary instruction, cooperative learning with students working in groups to produce a product, Close Reading, and Cornell Note-taking. All teachers are expected to utilize these strategies daily.

Jackson feels that motivating all stakeholders to live up to the mission and vision of the school is her most important responsibility. Connecting with teachers, parents, and students on a personal, face-to-face level helps her motivate everyone to support the plan for the school.

In addition to supportive parents and teachers, the surrounding community contributes to the school's success. On a Mission is an alternative-to-suspension program for students who exhibit defiant behavior or who commit a first offense. Edwin Henderson also provides mentoring for boys who are at risk of not fulfilling their potential. Counseling time is paid for through Rita Bright Davis, sending interns to work with students and plan activities like this year's Girls Day.

Ultimate Transformations provides healthy competition for after-school programs, training students on health and wellness while providing homework help. The Youth Policy Institute, which supplies their after-school program, donated a computer lab so that 125 students can participate in technology projects. At 4:00 p.m. each day, 180 Degrees feeds students participating in after-school programs.

However, the organization of the school day sets the tone for the school's culture. The school runs on a modified block schedule with six periods. There are sixty-minute periods Monday and Tuesday, fifty-five-minute periods on Wednesday due to an early out for teacher planning and professional development, and one hundred-minute blocks on Thursday and Friday where students attend even periods or three odd periods depending on the day of the week.

All students are enrolled in study hall, and all teachers tutor during that time. "The structure of the schedule has been the most important factor in creating a positive school culture," says Jackson. Even though electives were cut from the schedule this year due to budget constraints, the school still teaches rugby in PE, a sport that continues through high school.

Jackson makes the students line up before school starts and has her "fireside chats" in the morning when necessary. She spends most of her time in classrooms building good interpersonal relationships with students and staff. "We've bought into the belief that you have got to have a relationship with every child and parent in order to get the success you want," she remarked.

Students wear uniforms daily, and they must additionally wear ties Monday through Wednesday to solidify their self-image of scholarly professionalism. There are monthly rituals where students are honored for academic accomplishments and rewarded with lunch with the director. The school holds awards assemblies, oratorical contests, poetry readings, and other school-wide and class-specific activities to motivate and engage students in high achievement. The student body governing group, the Knight's Council, confers with the director, bringing a student voice to decisions and organizing activities for the school.

FUTURE PLANS

The future of View Park Preparatory Charter Middle School looks bright, and LAUSD has recently renewed their charter for the next five years. The school is working toward establishing a lasting, sustainable system at each grade level that does not depend on one or two veterans leading the way. The school continues on its path to realize its mission and vision, and Jackson is working to "really connect kids to outside resources and experiences because [she] wants them to be able to compete in the social experience that has nothing to do with X times Y."

The school plans to set goals on citizenship and what that means to individuals at each grade level, instilling in students the concept of civic duty and community service. The staff believes that this element will support their goal of creating a private education in a public school.

Academically, the school has adopted the Common Core standards and is in the process of bringing their curriculum in line with them. The school has also begun a push to engage students in the use of technology. They have begun by procuring Revolution Prep licenses for every child within the school day as well as creating projects and assessments using technology. The school has met their most recent AYP and increased math scores in grades seven and eight. They have also reduced their suspension rate by 60 percent.

Finally, the school has made reflection central; it guides planning for the present and future. Jackson has brought the Critical Friends concept to her faculty to help teachers improve their practice. This is a school where the adults are on the same page due to strong leadership and consistent communication between stakeholders.

CONCLUSIONS

View Park is a school that seeks to transform impoverished African American children into college-ready scholars. Their mission, to provide a private-school experience for their students, has guided the school toward adopting many effective strategies. View Park continues to modify its ways of working so that their mission is fully realized.

The mantra parents and staff repeat chorally at meetings is: "We are in a process; we are not perfect, but we strive for excellence." This concept truly characterizes the school culture at View Park as they continue to grapple with the challenges they have embraced.

KEY ELEMENTS

- A weekly school schedule that accommodates intervention, enrichment, professional development, and quality time for instruction.
- Strong community and parent partnerships that support science and academics, intervention, sports, and the arts.
- A Saturday and after-school intervention program that addresses both academics and behavior.
- A safe, enclosed academic environment that promotes a college-going culture.

Part III

CHARTER HIGH SCHOOLS

CHAPTER 8

Bright Star Academy
Los Angeles, California

INTRODUCTION

Jeff Hilger, Founder of Bright Star Schools, became a Teach for America teacher in the Los Angeles Unified School District (LAUSD) in 1993, and taught in a South Los Angeles middle school for two years. While working as a substitute teacher, he completed a dual degree in law and urban planning from UCLA. While practicing law he worked on a project involving charter schools, which led to intensive research into KIPP (Knowledge Is Power Program), a charter school operator.

While still at the law firm, he wrote the grant that became Bright Star Schools. There was a church in the West Adams area of Los Angeles with an empty school building, and a community hungry for new educational options. As Mr. Hilger puts it, "Basically it was me seeing it as an opportunity and missing being in education." The school opened with one fifth-grade and two sixth-grade classes in 2003.The school grew about a hundred students each year and added grade levels until the high school was opened in 2006.

Currently, fifth and sixth grades are still housed at the West Adams church site (Stella Charter Middle Academy), while the seventh through twelfth grades (Bright Star Charter Academy) are housed at a closed LAUSD elementary site in Westchester. The seventh- and eighth-grade students are considered part of Stella Charter Middle Academy although housed in Westchester, and have their own county-district-school (CDS) code.

As a young school, Bright Star Secondary Academy has garnered numerous awards including: number one performing charter school in

LAUSD (California Charter Schools Association, 2008), California Title I Distinguished School (California Department of Education, 2009), and California Distinguished School Award (California Department of Education, 2011). Considering demographically similar schools, Bright Star is ranked highly among LAUSD high schools.

According to Marni Parsons, Student Services Manager, "We run a pretty tight ship. The founder's vision was for it to be like an academy—almost like a military academy. Students wear uniforms and there are very rigid expectations for behavior as well as how you do your work with integrity."

The ethnic breakdown of Bright Star's ninth- to twelfth-grade students is 3 percent Asian/Filipino/Pacific Islander, 76 percent Hispanic, and 13 percent African American. Approximately 94 percent of the students are on the Free and Reduced-Price Lunch Program (Socioeconomically Disadvantaged), 15 percent are ELs, and 10 percent are SWDs.

Bright Star's API rose from 762 in 2006/2007 to 870 in 2012/2013. The school met thirteen of thirteen AYP goals, and remains free of the No Child Left Behind Program Improvement status.

There is accountability on the teachers' part to maintain high standards. At the beginning of each school year, teachers do comparisons

Data Implications

			Ethnicity			
Year	Enrollment	% AI	% Asian/Filipino/ Pacific Islander	% Black	% Hispanic	% White
2012–13	432	0.2	2.5	12.5	76.1	0.5
2010–11	351	0	2.3	13.4	83.8	0.6
2010–11	246	0	1.6	12.6	85.4	0

Year	% Socioeconomic	% English Learners	% Students w/ Disabilities
2012–13	93.8	15.3	10.1
2011–12	82.9	25.9	3.4
2010–11	89.8		

Year	API	% AYP—English Lang Arts*	% Mathematics*
2012–13	807	67.8	68.6
2011–12	820	72.3	67.8
2010–11	838	90.5	92.9

* = Percent at/above Proficient

of students' grades with scores on standardized tests. Students who are passing a class but failing on the standardized test (or vice versa) indicate a problem to be examined. For example, if a student gets a "B" in a class, but gets a Below Basic on the STAR (Standardized Testing and Reporting) test, that "B" converts to an incomplete.

The students can then clear that incomplete in four ways: (a) retaking the class; (b) taking an SAT2 and getting a score of proficient; (c) using the Study Island computer program to prove mastery; or (d) taking an online class. When the students have satisfied one of these options to proficiency, they can raise the incomplete grade to a C+. This system has the added benefit that students understand that the test matters to them personally, and therefore take it seriously and try their best.

Regardless of the student's score on the STAR, any student who receives less than a 75 percent in class does not receive credit for the class. Students in the range of 70 to 75 percent are considered incompletes. Unless they are able to show mastery by test, Study Island, or their finals and midterms, they must retake the class. Any student who receives less than 70 percent must retake the class.

As Principal Monique Bonilla elaborates, "We are looking at standard-based grading and standard-based teaching so that students get the opportunity to take that standard over before moving on to the next standard instead of, let's say, average all the grades together and give a 'C' in the class.

"Teaching is based on key standards and students are given multiple opportunities to pass the test. This is a lot of work for the teacher; they have to create multiple tests and they have to reteach. The hardest part is logistics—they must have groups and stations. Teachers have to own it. They can't say, 'I rocked it,' but 80 percent of the students failed." She further reflects, "This means owning the most difficult kids and reflecting and recognizing where you're failing, and where you need to improve and be humble enough to say, OK, this is where I messed up and this is where I need to do it again."

By eliminating social promotion, students are held accountable for what they know. As Tatiana Mirzaian, math teacher, states, "If they don't master the skills they need in pre-algebra, they stay in pre-algebra until they do. So when they do get to the higher-level classes, it's expected for them to be able to not only understand what needs to happen in that class, but also be pushed to the next level and understand all aspects of the class. That allows the teachers to be able to push the rigor to a higher level because the students coming in are more prepared."

Jane Han, math teacher, concurs, "It's the school's philosophy and the flexibility of the school allows that. It's being OK with difficult situations. There's the willingness to have these very detailed, complex plans and be flexible with situations. It creates more work for teachers and administrators, but we're willing to do it."

With the lack of social promotion come challenges. Corey Taylor, science teacher, clarifies, "The culture of the school changes when students other than from Stella come in—students who have been socially promoted. Incoming students who have passed algebra 1 expect to move on, but we put them in the pre-algebra. We give entrance exams for math and English to place students in the correct classes."

Each teacher develops a standards map for the year and daily lesson plans that are submitted to administration for approval. Benchmark assessments (midterms and finals) are created using teacher-created questions and questions from Data Director.

Available to students is "I work" (independent work that includes time for homework and tutoring). There is free tutoring before school starting at 7:00 a.m., and after school from 3:30 p.m. (Bright Star has a longer school day) to 4:30 p.m., which is mandatory for the students who are struggling. In the morning, math and English are provided to students in small groups of six to eight. In the afternoon, all teachers have their doors open for tutoring, so the students can self-select where they need the most help. To ensure that tutoring takes precedence, sports and other enrichment activities do not start until 4:30 p.m.

SUCCESS FACTORS

Starting in tenth grade, high-achieving students have the opportunity to attend West Los Angeles Community College to earn college credit. According to Mr. Hilger, high achieving does not necessarily mean straight-A students. Rather, students who are at least solid B students and are willing to put in the work are part of the program. Approximately 50 percent, ninety students, in grades ten through twelve participate. Students are only allowed to take college transferable classes—the goal being that students earn sixty college units and then transfer to a university as a junior. Students are not encouraged to earn an associate's degree as many of those classes do not transfer.

Students have the opportunity to remain at Bright Star for a fifth year to improve their grade-point average or SAT scores. Mr. Hilger likens this to a finishing school back East where students can improve their college package. "So we have kids who could graduate from the lower bar, with a 3.0, but they say, 'I'm going to stick around to get a 3.5 and take higher-level math, higher-level science,' and we say fine—do it—because that's what rich kids do. If they're not ready for Columbia, they go to Choate for a year and improve their grades. It's called prep year. Twenty to 30 percent of Ivy League acceptances come from a prep year. So if they're doing it, why aren't we doing it? Our kids are less ready than anybody, so if they're willing to stay in our program, and they can be at a community college, we can claim money to help them and we can support them."

Students can stay until their twenty-second birthday as long as they meet certain criteria: (a) They must be continuously enrolled (dual enrolled); (b) They must be taking enough units and making significant progress toward graduation. Once the student turns nineteen, the rigorous Bright Star graduation requirements no longer apply, and the students need only meet the LAUSD graduation requirements (A-G classes, 240 units). The University of California and the California State University system both require students successful completion of the A-G requirements. The only way to satisfy this requirement is to take and pass approved high school courses with a grade of "C" or better.

The graduation requirements at Bright Star Secondary Academy are unique. Students must meet the minimum A-G requirements, pass the CAHSEE (California High School Exit Exam), and pass a writing test. Students are required to take music, and must play a song on an instrument before they graduate. They must be able to run three miles in thirty minutes and complete two other physical challenges. They must have acceptance to at least two universities and a financial plan completed. This financial plan gives the students a realistic view of what college really costs.

Students are asked to reflect on the fact that even if they have scholarships and grants, there is a cost to travel, cell phones, clothing, etc. They must have four semesters of extracurricular activities such as clubs, sports, or ASB (Associated Student Body), and at least fifty hours of community service in at least two organizations. They must visit at least ten universities and five national parks or historical sites, and attend five campfires (community builders). Juniors and seniors must take a financial literacy course at West LA College during the winter break. Students who are not making adequate progress on these requirements are required to take an additional course (Rite of Passage).

Students are required to read thirty minutes a day, 360 days a year, and earn points necessary for graduation. There is a required reading list which outlines the classics the students are required to read. Starting in seventh grade, students earn 175 points for reading twelve books which include classics such as *Treasure Island, Anne Frank: Diary of a Young Girl*, and *The Lion, the Witch and the Wardrobe*. A student in the twelfth grade must read seventeen books to earn four hundred points. These books include *Macbeth, The Sound and the Fury, The Autobiography of Malcolm X, Animal Farm, The Kite Runner*, and *Atlas Shrugged*, for example.

Some of these selections are covered in class; others are considered independent reading and the students' responsibility. Students must fill out a reading log and write a summary of the book before taking the Reading Counts test (Scholastic). The books are all provided to the students, and their scores/points go into teachers' grade books to help with accountability.

Recognizing that not all students will be part of the University Prep program (UP), there is a track of students (Choice Academy, [CA]) who have slightly different requirements for graduation. Students in UP must pass all courses with a "B" or better, while students in the CA must have a "C" or better in all courses. The students in CA do not have the same required-books reading list, nor must they have university acceptances.

Bright Star's Life Experience Lessons (LELs) provide the means for students to meet several of the graduation requirements. These are opportunities for students to take both day trips and overnight trips. The day trips may include excursions that include hiking, biking, beach cleanups, museum visits, and cultural plays and concerts. The overnight trips include national parks, historical landmarks, and university visits.

The twelfth-grade culminating trip is determined by the students—the graduating class of 2012 visited Puerto Rico. Students must earn the privilege of attending these trips by maintaining a high "accountability score." This score includes grades, behavior, reading points, physical education, benchmark assessments, and meeting deadlines. Students always know where they are with their accountability scores, which helps them to stay on track and hold themselves accountable.

Rather than a dean of discipline or a detention room, there is a "connector" who oversees the Connecting Place (CP). The CP is both a physical room and a philosophy where students and teachers resolve conflict outside of the classroom, ensuring that valuable learning is not disrupted or lost because of problem behavior. The philosophy for this program comes from William Glasser in his "Quality Schools" work, which states when a student misbehaves there is a disconnect in a relationship. Teachers use typical classroom-management strategies that sometimes do not work, and then the disconnect causes problems for the entire classroom.

When this occurs, students are sent to the CP so they have some time to reflect on their behavior in the class. The students write a reflection (their version of the story), and the connector has a discussion with the student to discuss the student's goals, what they need to stop doing, and what they need to start doing. The teacher then comes at the end of the class to ascertain where the disconnect occurred and how to repair the relationship. The connector serves as a mediator between the student and teacher to ensure that the conversation is about the behavior, and not a reprimand.

There are no out-of-school suspensions—all suspensions are in school, in the CP. Work is obtained from all the classes, and the connector is there to supervise and provide support. If a student is sent to the CP, his or her connector immediately receives an e-mail that there is a student waiting for their support. The discipline program is very specific on the infractions that require the CP. For example, students are not sent to the CP for a uniform violation or for chewing gum. If it's a fixable problem, the students may be sent to the CP to fix it and then return to class (e.g., removing fingernail polish).

FUTURE PLANS

Jeff Hilger shares, "A lot of different people have asked us to grow. I have the money in the bank, but I'm being very cautious." He continues, "If you look at the big Charter Management Organizations (CMO), that's part of the reason we made the decision to grow really slowly. There's a lot of new schools' venture-fund money that came in that said build ten schools in ten years, and that doesn't work very well." Currently he is looking for a project to build a permanent home for the elementary school. Rise, a new middle school in Koreatown, is opening with 150 sixth graders and will grow from there. Responding to the community desire for a school, the school will be housed at a church location that encompasses the entire city block. Ultimately the goal is to move the high school closer to that location.

Bright Star is also exploring moving eight of their classrooms to the college campus so the students don't have to take a bus back and forth. Bright Star teachers will be housed there so that when the students are not in their college classes, they will be able to take their regular high school classes at the same location.

Currently parents have the ability to use the Internet to see their students' behavior, attendance, missing assignments, and grades in the Aeries Student Information System. Parents and students are asked to access the system weekly and discuss the student's status. The school is exploring systems to provide more options to parents such as receiving an automatic e-mail when any data on their students undergo a change.

CONCLUSIONS

Bright Star Secondary Academy has a proven success record by offering students a rigorous, college preparatory program in concert with life experiences that broaden their horizons. Its unique partnership with West LA College, and the structure that allows students an additional prep year for college, have created a pathway to success not afforded elsewhere in public education. Students have an innovative support system in the Connecting Place, which ensures that they are getting the most of an exceptional program.

Monique Bonilla sums it up, "There is a lot of need. That's what I love about this school. A lot of our students have parents that might not be educated, but they know they want something better for their kids. So they've chosen to bring them to a charter school, and they've chosen us. Some of those kids work so hard and they want it. This is giving them the opportunity to have that private education, but public, because they couldn't afford to do it otherwise."

KEY ELEMENTS

- Students must demonstrate proficiency in subjects before they are allowed to move on. There is no social promotion.
- Students are responsible for completing graduation requirements that exceed those of the Los Angeles Unified School District.
- A partnership with the local community college provides opportunities for students to earn college credits that transfer to four-year colleges and/or universities.
- Students are allowed to complete a fifth year of high school to improve their standing before entering college.

CHAPTER 9

Environmental Science and Technology High School
Los Angeles, California

INTRODUCTION

The LAUSD school reform movements of the 1990s have been realized in Alliance Environmental Science and Technology High School (ESAT). The measured hand of experience has crafted an oasis of learning in this glistening glass and steel structure set in the Glassell Park neighborhood northwest of the Los Angeles civic center. The veteran LAUSD educators who created the Alliance for College-Ready Public Schools brought forth this successful school model in part through the strong partnerships they established over time with the community and Los Angeles business.

The story of ESAT really began with LEARN (Los Angeles Educational Alliance for Restructuring Now) and LAAMP (Los Angeles Annenberg Metropolitan Project), two powerful motivations for dedicated educators who wanted more local control for schools in order to better serve students.

Former principal Howard Lappin was best known for taking Foshay Middle School from the lowest rung of the LAUSD achievement ladder and moving the school to national prominence for academic success. In 1989 Foshay was ranked among the thirty-one lowest-performing LAUSD schools. Lappin and his staff transformed Foshay into a learning center, earning the California Distinguished School designation by 1996.

"I ultimately ran Foshay like a charter school," remembers Lappin.

The mission of Alliance for College-Ready Public Schools is to open and operate a network of small high-performing (secondary) schools in historically underachieving, low-income communities in California that will annually demonstrate student academic achievement growth and graduate students ready for success in college. The Alliance is led by Judy Burton, another former LAUSD teacher, principal, local district superintendent, and assistant superintendent of the Office of School Reform.

Governed by board members such as William G. Ouchi of UCLA, former mayor Richard Riordan, ambassador Frank Baxter, as well as other powerful Los Angeles leaders, Alliance has grown to seventeen high schools and nine middle schools, all out-performing their LAUSD counterparts. Even Bill Gates has been impressed by Alliance's progress, touting BLAST (Blending Learning for Alliance School Transformation) in a 2012 speech about technology use in education. The BLAST model utilizes three learning stations, where students rotate from a teacher-led small group, to individual online learning, to collaborative groups during a two-hour block of time.

According to Lappin, Alliance sets the rules, the guidelines, and the expectations, and gives principals the freedom to achieve the goals of the school. Alliance secures the buildings, allocates funding to run the schools, and does much of the paperwork and reports for the state and federal government. Due to the deep community support that Alliance leadership has maintained over the years, much of the Alliance's funding comes from private donors. These relationships and the experienced educators running the Alliance are its formula for success.

The school lives up to its name. "This is a green school; a LEED (Leadership in Energy and Environmental Design) Gold Medallion site," Lappin stated. Students can take UC-approved environmental science in the tenth grade. Recycling and sustainability are evident all over the campus. The site itself utilizes solar panels to produce carbon-free electricity. The mission of the school is in keeping with the goals of Alliance: In preparations for their future college careers and beyond, ESAT will support the development of academically successful and ethical learners who understand their impact and influence on the community and environment.

ESAT opened in 2009 with 192 ninth-grade students, growing to a total school population of 549 in grades nine to twelve by spring 2013. They graduated their first class in 2013. ESAT's API was 860 in 2013. They are rated ten in both state and similar schools' rankings.

Data Implications

Year	Enrollment	% AI	% Asian/Filipino/ Pacific Islander	% Black	% Hispanic	% White
			Ethnicity			
2012–13	549	0.2	7.3	1.5	89.1	1.8
2011–12	457	0	6.3	1.3	88.6	3.3
2010–11	286	0	5.2	1.4	87.1	1.4

Year	% Socioeconomic	% English Learners	% Students w/ Disabilities
2012–13	89.4	6.6	3.9
2011–12	90.6	11.2	3.5
2010–11	90.9	15.7	8.1

Year	API	% AYP—English Lang Arts*	% Mathematics*
2012–13	860	76.9	82.2
2011–12	871	66.7	77.8
2010–11	881	81.2	83.8

* = Percent at/above Proficient

This standing can be attributed to achievement growth in the Hispanic, Socioeconomically Disadvantaged, and English-learner student populations.

The school's enrollment consists of 89 percent Hispanic, 7 percent Asian/Filipino/Pacific Islander, 2 percent African American, and 2 percent White. Eighty-nine percent are Socioeconomically Disadvantaged, 4 percent are SWDs, 7 percent are ELs, and 48 percent are Reclassified Fluent English Proficient.

In some ways it is difficult to compare ESAT with nearby LAUSD schools, in part because many of its students come from places outside a traditional attendance area. However, ESAT's 860 API outpaces nearby Irving Middle School's 729, Franklin High School's 703, and Eagle Rock High School's 776.

Breaking down the data, ESAT's English-language arts, math, science, and history/social science scores average over 70 percent proficient-advanced, more than twenty points higher than LAUSD. The pass rate for the California High School Exit Exam is 100 percent in math and 98 percent in English. While there is no graduation information available yet, the school does have an impressively small dropout rate of 2.2 percent, which is better than LAUSD at 6.4 percent and the state at 4.6 percent.

In 2011, for the first time at ESAT, twenty-seven students took the environmental science Advanced Placement (AP) exam and forty-one passed in keeping with the school's mission to prepare students for the rigors of college. Since then, ESAT has provided AP calculus AB, AP biology, AP French, AP language and composition, AP literature, AP prep seminar, AP U.S. history, and AP government, with over 60 percent of the 161 students tested passing. In addition the school offers honors tenth-grade English, honors chemistry, honors world history, and recently added AP French and AP modern European history.

"Our data is excellent. We live on data," commented Lappin. The Alliance supports their schools by providing standards-based benchmarks for each course, given three times a year, thus providing their schools the opportunity to assess teaching and learning. The data are collected and analyzed, as are the tests themselves. Lappin summed it up: "Our assessments are wonderful because we have great teachers."

SUCCESS FACTORS

The success of ESAT starts with the clear mission and vision that it communicates to students, teachers, and parents. In order to prepare students for college success, ESAT, under the direction of the Alliance, operates under a core education model that focuses on five core values: (1) high expectations for all students; (2) small, personalized schools and classrooms; (3) increased instructional time; (4) highly qualified principals and teachers; and (5) parents as partners.

"How do you communicate the mission and vision?" asked Lappin. "It's posted, we talk to parents about it, it's communicated when we send out recruitment letters. We live it more than anything else."

From the professionally equipped fitness rooms with elliptical machines, treadmills, and free weights, to the spacious classrooms and hallways, the school lives up to its promises. All teachers use the same format for posting their agendas, focusing on lesson objectives, standards, classwork, and homework, creating a continuity that establishes positive routines.

Even their school uniforms bring a controlled, professional quality to the atmosphere of the school, with students wearing different-colored shirts as they progress from grade to grade. Students must earn enough credits to wear the color of their class, and this policy has proven helpful in motivating students to keep up with their studies.

The school even requires ten more credits for a diploma than does LAUSD. "You can see I'm really very strict and I don't put up with any nonsense; I'm too old!" stated Lappin. "I tell the kids, I'm going to tell you how to dress, I'm going to tell you how to behave, I'm going to tell you what classes to take, and I will get you into college. That's, in essence, what we are." These high expectations for behavior and academic achievement create a positive environment at the school. "I don't think the kids feel oppressed here. It's a free and easygoing atmosphere," said Lappin.

The school's success can be directly attributed to this atmosphere and the consideration the administration and staff has for the attitudes of its students. ESAT has opened a leadership class that is very active in creating activities for the student body. Athletics also engage students in soccer, softball, baseball, cross-country, volleyball, basketball, and cheerleading, with the school using local public facilities for practice and games.

Students can enroll in college classes after school and in the summer programs taught on campus. Through the environmental science program, students work with the Friends of the Los Angeles River, Tree People, and other local groups to clean up the community. The school also has a partnership with Occidental College's Science on the Road program to support student interest and achievement in environmental and other sciences.

ESAT students meet in an advisory period for forty-five minutes four times a week with a college-ready curriculum that is grade-level specific. Because the school saw an interest and a need for the Advancement Via Individual Determination (AVID) program, the school has opened up an AVID elective to support students. The school also offers the California State University Expository Reading and Writing Course for its seniors choosing not to take Advanced Placement English literature. In short, as a need or interest arises, the school is quick to embark on a new direction to best support its students.

The school day is maximized for student achievement. School begins at 7:45 a.m. and ends at 3:30 p.m., longer than most local schools, and the school year begins in early August and extends to June, a full two weeks longer than LAUSD. The school utilizes a block schedule, rotating even and odd periods, and reverses the order of classes so that students can meet their French class, for example, on Monday in the morning and on Thursday in the afternoon—an accommodation they find gives both teachers and students a more engaging opportunity to teach and learn. The school also pays teachers to tutor students after school.

Where most high schools offer several foreign language options, ESAT only offers French. Lappin explains, "The first reason is the non-Spanish speakers here are all either Afro-American, Anglo, or Asian, and the Spanish speakers are all Hispanic. That separation of a racially based class (Spanish for Spanish speakers) affects every other class because students tend to cluster a little bit. Secondly, we thought it would be a little fun to have everybody on an even playing field; a fresh start for everybody."

The mission of ESAT dictates that all students enroll in A-G requirement courses as preparation for admission to the University of California campuses. Student schedules are standard, with electives available in the twelfth grade only. Students take physical education only in the ninth grade. The school uses an inclusion model for English learners, students with disabilities, and gifted. "We don't pull out English Learners, we work with them," said Lappin. The school has two resource teachers who work inside classrooms with SWDs and others who need assistance.

Yet the most important factor in the success of ESAT is staffing. "Staffing is key," said Lappin. "I look for somebody with a belief system that inner-city kids are going to learn and go to college. This is a hard school to work at. There are very high expectations. The scores are obviously very high, we're very successful, and the teachers load that on themselves."

When interviewing candidates, Lappin's assistant principal asks the instructional questions and Lappin looks for the response and commitment. Once a teacher is hired, the school provides supportive professional development and training, as well as grade-level and course-specific collaboration. The school has a few staff members from Teach for America, and seven teachers have followed Lappin from previous schools. The school works to give teachers as few preparations as possible so that each teacher can be an expert in the courses they teach.

Professional development occurs every Wednesday and is a collaborative effort involving the teachers and the assistant principal. In fact, teachers' ideas and opinions are an important factor in decision making. Lappin illustrated this fact by recalling the first year of the school, when the Alliance felt the KIPP schools model of a 7:45 a.m. to 4:30 p.m. school day would optimize learning. Teachers soon voiced their frustration at feeling burned out and so the schedule was changed.

"We didn't change the ending time for kids because you can't do that," said Lappin. "We had an hour study hall, where teachers had nothing to do but just sit there and grade papers; we also rotated teachers so they could leave early. This decision came from them and we were able to change things due to that flexibility as a charter school."

In support of good teaching, the Alliance has become a part of The College-Ready Promise (TCRP), funded by the Bill and Melinda Gates Foundation. According to its website, this coalition of California public charter-management organizations hopes to implement an innovative plan to attract and retain highly effective teachers to work with students and dramatically increase the number of college-ready graduates.

This process not only serves to evaluate the performance of teachers, it also provides growth opportunities so teachers can improve. Rubrics and observation tools help administrators and teachers focus on good teaching, and information from observations and student achievement is captured in a database. In addition, videos and professional-development opportunities are connected to the website so teachers can learn effective teaching strategies and methods to engage and challenge all learners.

According to Lappin, "Ultimately, the results will be part of the pay. We're going to go to differentiated pay, so that's a part of it. There is also a survey of kids and test scores and growth—annual yearly growth." The Alliance teachers are very involved in the TCRP process and spend much of their professional development time defining what it takes to be college-ready.

To sum up his experience in education, Lappin feels that administrators need to have experience in the classroom. "It's critical," he said. "You really need to understand teaching and how that works and be very competent. Teachers need to see that you are competent."

FUTURE PLANS

For the immediate future, ESAT graduated its first class in spring 2013. In support of this first group's success in college, the school has implemented writing across the curriculum and is working to bring its students to higher competency in college-level writing. With its hard-working staff and devoted leadership, ESAT is well on its way to realizing its mission.

To ensure continued success, the school would like to involve its parents at a higher level. While parents participate in advisory councils, parent conferencing, workshops, and other school activities, ESAT continues to look for ways to engage parents in a meaningful way to support their students' achievement.

The school's college counselor works with the elected parent coordinator to educate parents on college-related issues like financial aid and admissions policies. The goal of the school is that at least 60 percent of their parents attend parent workshops, 80 percent complete at least twenty volunteer hours, and 75 percent attend parent-teacher conferences throughout the year.

Finally, the school hopes to continue in its facility and secure a long-term lease. "The Alliance is committed to the community," said Lappin. Wherever the school physically resides, ESAT will provide its students with the tools they need to prepare them for success in college and beyond, with the skills and experience to live in and contribute to a sustainable economy.

CONCLUSIONS

ESAT has been a success, as have all of the Alliance schools, primarily due to the teaching and administrative experience of its founders and current leaders. Not only have they drawn upon past reform efforts, but they have continued to fine-tune policies and programs to create an extremely high-functioning academic environment for traditionally underserved students.

This type of charter school organization is somewhat unique since it began with seasoned educators deeply rooted in one of the largest school districts in the country. Their firsthand experience has given them the insight and skill to craft a smaller, effective, twenty-first-century school "district" that continues to flourish.

KEY ELEMENTS

- Consistent, experienced leadership at the central office and local school.
- Committed community partners, garnered by the Alliance, that provide substantial financial support.
- Clear expectations that each student will graduate college-ready and focused on environmental science and technology.
- A consistent school culture that establishes positive routines.
- Highly effective teachers who serve as experts in their subject field.

CHAPTER 10

Dr. Olga Mohan High School
Los Angeles, California

INTRODUCTION

Geographically, Alliance Dr. Olga Mohan High School (DOMHS) could not exist in a more unlikely setting. Standard-issue LAUSD portable bungalows sit on asphalt, arranged in tight rows nestled in the southeast intersection of the Santa Monica and Harbor Freeways. The overhead sounds of racing cars maneuvering the freeway interchange compete with street-level trailer-trucks moving new cars to and from the lot across the street, and storage buildings and small industrial businesses surround the campus.

In keeping with the philosophy behind all Alliance schools, "The mission and vision of this school is to get our kids not only into college but to make sure they are successful in college and graduate within four years," according to Principal Janette Rodriguez. She personally promises each parent and student that her school will offer a quality education to ensure graduation from high school in four years and success in college. "When you sign up for this school," she said, "you sign up for getting kids into college."

The Alliance supports the campus and principal in operational areas as well as in curriculum and instruction. Principals are empowered to make instructional decisions on their own in the best interests of their school and within the mission and vision of the Alliance. This principal empowerment allows each Alliance school to find and utilize what works for them. In terms of budget, the Alliance takes care of each school's needs by working with the principal to prioritize expenditures.

"I tell them what our needs are," Rodriguez stated, "and they tell me 'yes' or 'no.' If I have a need and I can't afford it, I find out if I need to bring in more students or cut in another area." Principals work with Alliance's budget team throughout the year to keep schools on track regarding expenses. Because Average Daily Attendance (ADA) is the primary funding source for DOMHS, enrollment and attendance are closely monitored.

The strong foundation that has kept the school's mission clearly in the minds of its stakeholders began with an emphasis on school culture. "The former principal was adamant that our first focus would be school culture," said Rodriguez. "His philosophy was that a school cannot have good, sound instruction without a positive school culture first. That's been what we've always done, because it worked."

The supportive relationships between staff members, students, and parents have been a cornerstone for the school's success and it was primarily because of these relationships that Rodriguez, the former assistant principal, agreed to lead the school when the founding principal was promoted to the Alliance home office.

Data Implications

			Ethnicity			
Year	Enrollment	% AI	% Asian/Filipino/ Pacific Islander	% Black	% Hispanic	% White
2012–13	458	0	0.7	1.5	97.8	0
2011–12	444	0	0.7	2.9	95.0	1.4
2010–11*	435	0	0	3.7	72.4	0.2

* = 23% not reported

Year	% Socioeconomic	% English Learners	% Students w/ Disabilities
2012–13	98.7	12.2	7.4
2011–12	98.9	16.4	6.0
2010–11	98.2	18.2	5.3

Year	API	% AYP—English Lang Arts*	% Mathematics*
2012–13	895	66.7	97.2
2011–12	883	60.0	92.2
2010–11	894	80.0	97.3

* = Percent at/above Proficient

"We built such a great relationship with the students and the staff that I just couldn't let someone else take over," she stated. This continuity in management is an important factor that makes DOMHS a success.

Most of the students attending DOMHS come from the surrounding neighborhoods, though each year the school has been attracting more students from outside the traditional attendance area. On the surface, the demographics of its 458-member student body are in many ways similar to the three nearest LAUSD high schools, with less than 1 percent Asian/Pacific Islander, 2 percent African American, 98 percent Hispanic, and 99 percent Socioeconomically Disadvantaged.

However, the similarities end when looking at EL and SWD data. Santee (enrollment 2,900) has 12 percent SWDs and 38 percent ELs, West Adams (enrollment 2,500) has 13 percent SWDs and 35 percent ELs, and Jefferson (enrollment 1,960) has 13 percent SWDs and 37 percent ELs compared to the much smaller percentages at DOMHS with 7 percent SWDs and 12 percent ELs.

With an API score of 895, DOMHS far surpasses its three neighboring LAUSD high schools, with Santee at 636, West Adams at 646, and Jefferson at 601. The strong college prep program is also reflected in the tenth-grade California High School Exit Exam data, which show 95 percent of DOMHS's students passing the English section and 99 percent on the math section, compared to the local LAUSD high school scores which range from a 48 percent to 63 percent pass rate.

In 2013 100 percent of DOMHS's seniors met all graduation requirements (UC/CSU A-G requirements) and 99 percent were accepted into a two- or four-year college. A look at the data from the local LAUSD schools paints a very different picture: Jefferson High shows 34 percent completed the A-G requirements and 47 percent graduated; Santee shows 24 percent completed A-G and 54 percent graduated; and West Adams shows 32 percent completed A-G and 70 percent graduated.

In addition to these data points, DOMHS collects assessment data throughout the school year and utilizes them to support each student. The school has a data director who inputs the data from Alliance-created benchmark assessments given quarterly and works with teachers to create reports that illustrate how students are performing.

The school also carefully studies the results of SATs, ACTs, and AP exams in addition to state assessments. The school offers AP classes in biology, calculus AB, English language, English literature, Spanish language, Spanish literature, statistics, and United States history, and all students are required to take at least one AP class before graduating.

Perhaps the most important use of data by this school is its standards-based grading system, brought about in the second year as a response to the discrepancy between course grades and standardized test scores. The school has divided the state standards to fit into each semester for each class and no standard is weighted more than another. In grade books, student scores are by standard, not by assignment.

"There are different ways to assess mastery of the standards," commented Rodriguez. "A teacher can assess a particular standard through an exit slip, a unit test, an essay, a project. They have flexibility in the way they assess each standard." This stress on standards mastery over assignment completion helps students and teachers understand where students truly are in relation to the knowledge and skills they need to be college ready.

Because grading is standards based, parents can easily see where students are deficient and "be on board with the school in doing whatever it takes" to bring students to mastery, according to the principal. Using this type of data, teachers can personalize the tutoring they provide after school and on weekends. It is this use of data and standards-based grading that keeps the course fail rate low, according to the principal.

SUCCESS FACTORS

Perhaps the biggest factor that leads to success for Alliance schools in general is the deep educational experience and commitment of its leadership. Alliance guides its principals but ultimately gives them the freedom to create an individual atmosphere that is unique to each school. The atmosphere at DOMHS is best described as warm, open, and familial. In relating the way its twenty-two teachers look at student achievement, Rodriguez commented, "It is rare that a student would be low in credits (and not promote to the next grade level at the end of each year). We don't work in a punitive system. Our school culture is like one big happy family."

She added that teachers work with students to get them caught up if they fall behind, usually staying beyond the 7:45 a.m. to 3:30 p.m.

school day to tutor and sponsor student sports and activities and often working on weekends, doing whatever it takes to bring them to proficiency. By starting with a supportive school culture as their first goal, DOMHS has managed to recruit and keep like-minded, dedicated teachers who believe in the school and its students.

Coupled with the hiring of a committed teaching staff, the school and the Alliance provide teacher support through summer training and ongoing professional development for all teachers. During the school year, teachers meet each Wednesday for PD as a staff, a department team, or a grade-level team.

"Our PD is guided by our data," said Rodriguez. "Whatever our data is saying needs to be the focus of our professional development work." Additionally this past summer, new teachers worked several mornings a week with lead teachers on instruction, then put what they learned into practice with the summer school students in the afternoon, according to Rodriguez. It was especially important for new hires to use the standards-based grading system and the summer gave them guided experience.

The Alliance additionally has deleted the D grade and is working toward bringing its schools into agreement about a common grading system. The Alliance provides pacing guides to support their teachers, based on the Common Core standards. Since the Alliance is a part of the Bill and Melinda Gates Foundation's The College-Ready Promise (TCRP), DOMHS has begun the teacher-evaluation process, featuring formal and informal evaluations, observations, rubrics, data analysis, and merit pay.

Teachers have access to the data portal providing videos and resources to support teacher growth. Rodriguez explained that, in the past, the Alliance has given teachers bonuses if the school reached their API goals and met their enrollment numbers. With TCRP in place, these bonuses are linked to teacher evaluations and student progress and distributed to individuals, not faculties.

Another contributor to the school's success is its philosophy that all students can meet the A-G requirements and graduate in four years college ready. The school operates on an inclusion system, where resource specialists co-teach with general education teachers. The same holds true for English learners. "We don't get many students who need ESL classes," stated Rodriguez, "though, in the past, we have definitely had students who need extra language support." The school works to provide all students with whatever extra help they need in order to master the rigorous coursework that will enable them to succeed in AP classes and college.

DOMHS's partnership with Loyola Marymount University is another major factor in the success of their school. LMU supplies two faculty members who teach honors precalculus and biology and serve as model teachers for the Center for Math and Science Teachers program (CMAST) utilized by the school.

Originally, DOMHS's science and math teachers received training from LMU on teaching strategies to support achievement in math and science, but the rest of the faculty has seen the positive results and are using these strategies in other subject areas. The program requires teachers and students to use extensive data analysis to foster a deep understanding of both content and concept.

"In our classrooms students are engaged in conversations, participating at different learning stations, and working in groups on standards they might be struggling with," according to Rodriguez. This type of classroom differentiates instruction and has helped DOMHS's students move forward.

Student support is another contributor to the positive school culture that drives this school's accomplishments. In addition to a rigorous academic program with excellent teachers, DOMHS's students attend an advisory class for forty-five minutes four days a week with Alliance-designed standards and curriculum crafted for each grade level. Former students return from college to talk to the student body about their experiences and the importance of developing skills now for success later.

School-spirit activities, prom, field trips, and other student body undertakings are organized by students and teachers and supported by fund-raising at the school site. "Every year we get the In-and-Out truck to celebrate our successes," mentioned the principal. "We make sure we include students in our celebrations and get to know them on a more personal level."

The partnership with the Youth Policy Institute additionally creates after-school programs like a marathon running club, volleyball, soccer, band, and tutoring, and it pays teachers for their time. The school's two counselors have worked with local businesses and colleges to secure internships for students at places like the Museum of Science and Industry. The school sends students to summer programs around the state to broaden their knowledge base about the world around them.

"When asked where they want to go to college," said Rodriguez, "they always say USC and UCLA because they don't know that there's more out there." By working with CSU Los Angeles and CSU Northridge, for example, students can gain an understanding of the many quality institutions they can attend after high school graduation. The school's counselors also sign students up for community college concurrent enrollment.

In order to provide physical education to its students, the school has converted one of its classrooms into a fitness center through the help of Sound Body, Sound Mind. However, due to the physical nature of the school and its location, there were few opportunities for students to engage in sport.

"Mayor Riordan came one day and saw our kids playing basketball with a makeshift basketball court that was held up by trashcans," remembers Rodriguez. "He generously donated an actual basketball court that also doubles as a volleyball court." The school regularly has student versus staff volleyball and basketball games throughout the year in addition to the after-school programs and teams.

The school also partners with its parents by hosting monthly workshop meetings and parent advisory meetings. At these meetings, the school presents relevant data on the school and encourages parents to weigh in on school-wide policies, activities, concerns, and issues. The school's leadership students play an important role in these meetings, often presenting issues and asking for parents to help.

Families are encouraged, not required, to volunteer forty hours of community service per year, earning hours by attending meetings, participating in Back-to-School Night, conferring with teachers, and volunteering in classrooms and in the office. "The most important role parents can play is to work collaboratively with us in making sound instructional decisions for their children," said Rodriguez. "We encourage parents to both come in and participate in the most meaningful things like the workshops, parent conferences, and individual meetings with our teachers or administration."

FUTURE PLANS

With the strength of the Alliance network of schools and the success of DOMHS, the future seems bright. This school has taken on some of the city's most challenged students and has made good on its promise to prepare and graduate them ready for success in college. Rodriguez offers this advice to anyone hoping to replicate its story.

"Expect to do whatever it takes to get the job done," she said. "If that means sharpening pencils the day before benchmark administration then that's what you are doing. You serve lunch, you nurse kids, you do whatever it takes."

The school's future plans are mainly to continue the work they have been doing and fulfill the mission of preparing students for future success. "We've had three graduating classes," she said. "We've seen many of our students go off to college but are not long enrolled in a four-year school. Our biggest goal is to make sure our kids are successful, and have the necessary skills to be successful in college."

This school has made it clear to its graduates that they are welcomed to return at any time for the same kind of support that guided them to high school graduation in their pursuit of a college degree, whether it's help with coursework or with filling out financial aid forms. "If they need help three years down the road, "she added, "this is the place they can come to for help and support." That familial sentiment extends beyond graduation and will allow this school to accomplish its mission.

CONCLUSIONS

The success of this school is based on the experience and support of the Alliance and its community partners, as well as a team of dedicated educators. Their innovative use of standards-based grading, something that seems so logical, has helped them focus on teaching and learning.

This school is physically a small place, yet this smallness has instilled in students, faculty, staff, and parents a true sense of common purpose. Students here are not lost in the shuffle of a larger place where anonymity is too common; rather everyone here is known and valued, mentored and tutored, so each can reach the goal of not just college acceptance, but college and career success.

KEY ELEMENTS

- A strong, experienced central leadership in the Alliance.
- A system of inclusion where attention is paid to each individual student and his or her needs.
- A small, close-knit faculty that utilizes school-wide instructional strategies.
- A clear mission articulated to create a college-going culture
- The school-wide use of a standards-based grading system.

CHAPTER 11

Port of Los Angeles High School
San Pedro, California

INTRODUCTION

The idea for the Port of Los Angeles High School (POLAHS) began in the San Pedro Chamber of Commerce as a downtown redevelopment and business stimulus opportunity. James Cross, the president of the chamber, Camilla Townsend, president of the Business and Education Committee and member of the Harbor Commission, and Sandy Bradley, member of the Chamber's Education Committee were instrumental in moving the conversation along based on the knowledge that San Pedro High School was severely overcrowded and on the verge of having to go year-round, and that the Port of Los Angeles provided a unique venue (Maritime Studies and International Business) for student success.

Members of the chamber used their business savvy and political connections to start the process of creating the school. The chamber received an investigatory grant from the state of California, and also pushed the port to contribute to the development of the community at large by purchasing the property where the school is currently located.

The school opened in 2005 with 112 ninth-grade students, four teachers, and a principal, and spent the first three months of its existence housed at the Boy Scout Camp at Cabrillo Beach. Since that time, the school has grown to 950 students, seventy teachers, administrators, and staff, and has graduated three senior classes. Students from twenty-one different middle schools from the communities of San Pedro, Wilmington, Lomita, Harbor City, Gardena, and Carson attend the school. The school is located in the port district of San Pedro and now owns part of a large complex, which also houses the Port of Los Angeles administration offices and the Los Angeles Port Police and Homeland Security divisions.

There is a business atmosphere with pristine hallways and classrooms designed around the subject being taught. In every classroom, unique colors, murals, art of the Port of Los Angeles, furniture, and equipment create an inviting environment for students. Teachers are clustered by department to assist in pacing coherence and to promote collegiality; classes are held to twenty-five or fewer students. It is clear that students and staff share great pride in their school. Although the school is in an area plagued by graffiti and vandalism, this is not a problem at POLAHS. The culture of the school is quickly embraced by incoming freshmen, and students become an integral part in maintaining a safe, clean, welcoming environment.

Professionalism is a cornerstone of that culture. Students wear uniforms, and teachers wear business attire. Every teacher is responsible for every student's behavior anywhere on campus. Even substitute teachers must participate in an orientation to ensure that they meet the same professional standards before they can work at POLAHS.

Data Implications

| Year | Enrollment | % AI | Ethnicity | | | |
			% Asian/Filipino/ Pacific Islander	% Black	% Hispanic	% White
2012–13	964	0.3	6.7	5.9	68.8	19.0
2011–12	933	0.6	6.6	6.4	66.6	19.2
2010–11	850	0.6	7.5	7.2	64.6	20.1

Year	% Socioeconomic	% English Learners	% Students w/ Disabilities
2012–13	38.9	2.2	8.2
2011–12	16.0	4.2	10.0
2010–11	16.5		6.3

Year	API	% AYP—English Lang Arts*	% Mathematics*
2012–13	834	83.8	84.3
2011–12	836	77.3	73.8
2010–11	791	68.7	71.4

* = Percent at/above Proficient

The ethnic breakdown of POLAHS's 950 students is 19 percent White, 7 percent Asian/Filipino/Pacific Islander, 69 percent Hispanic, and 6 percent African American. Approximately 39 percent of the students are on the Free and Reduced-Price Lunch Program (Socioeconomically Disadvantaged), 2 percent are ELs, and 8 percent are SWDs. It should be noted that since the school does not have a kitchen and does not provide meals, the percentage of Socioeconomically Disadvantaged is probably much higher since the majority of students were eligible for the Free and Reduced-Price Lunch program in their previous elementary and middle schools.

The school graduates more than 90 percent of its seniors, and more than 90 percent of sophomores pass the California High School Exit Exam (CAHSEE) on the first attempt. This can be attributed to the strong support given to students prior to taking the CAHSEE. Chariot software is used in math and English classes for two months preceding the test. Students take a pretest, and lower-scoring students are given supplementary tutoring and instruction.

POLAHS's API rose from 650 in 2006/2007 to 834 in 2012/2013. All test results (CST, CAHSEE, and AP) are analyzed by departments during a week-long summer institute held at the beginning of each school year. This annual "Maritime Institute," is sponsored by the Port of Los Angeles.

The standards-based assessments that are given every five weeks are scored through Data Director and, along with grades and other indicators of student achievement, are tracked through Aeries. Freshmen take diagnostic assessment exams in math, English, and science before entering, and are placed in the appropriate classes. If students are found to be too low, they are enrolled in a mandatory summer bridge program before entering ninth grade.

Analysis of these various data points provides a road map for professional development throughout the year. Areas of strength and weakness are identified by teachers to allow for sharing of best practices and to provide additional support where needed. In May, during CST testing, a "mini camp" is held during the three afternoons of testing. This is a time for intense reflection about the past year. Analysis of benchmark assessments helps create the agenda for the summer institute creating a constant recursive cycle of continuous improvement.

SUCCESS FACTORS

In order to reduce and lower the supervisory ratio to improve the quantity and quality of feedback given to teachers, the lead teacher program was implemented in the 2008/2009 school year. There are four lead teachers who have taken on the responsibilities of a second administrator. Each lead teacher directly supervises, supports, and evaluates the teachers on a grade level. Principal Gaetano (Tom) Scotti selects the lead teachers based on their experience and mastery of the California State Standards for the Teaching Profession.

As lead teacher Annie Reynolds puts it, "We are all very invested—we want to see our school get to a better place. We're leading the front of that, so it's an exciting place to be for us." Lead teacher Tim Dikdan adds, "Tom selects lead teachers based on the mastery of teaching—at the top of their game. But, don't call me a master teacher—I'm still learning. I go into classes and observe and see incredible things."

Lead teachers are given an extra conference period every day. According to lead teacher Don Ormsby, "I provide mentoring and support. I'm not here to criticize, I'm here to support. I tell my teachers at the beginning of the year that I'm looking for what's going right in the classroom and then if I see something that's an issue, we talk about it."

Lead teachers base their work with teachers on POLAHS's Four Pillars. These are:

- Classroom Management
  - Clear student and class expectations
  - On-task atmosphere
  - Effective transitions
  - Respect for teacher authority
  - Consistent enforcement of class rules
- Planning and Organization
  - Rigorous content
  - Standards based
  - Logical sequencing
  - Appropriate pacing
  - Frequent checks for understanding
  - Varied and meaningful assessments

- Student Interaction
  - Effective learning environment
  - All students engaged
  - All students dealt with fairly
  - Firm but fair individual student discipline
- Differentiated and Varied Instruction
  - Different learning styles
  - Scaffolding
  - Specially Designed Academic Instruction in English (SDAIE) methods targeted for all ELL students
  - Special-education accommodations
  - Use of technology

Teachers are visited by lead teachers frequently. However, for new teachers, the lead teacher and principal are in the classrooms more often. Both give the teacher feedback to ensure that students are aware of expectations even when the new teacher doesn't have all the management techniques mastered. The principal or lead teacher covers classes so that teachers may observe each other. Based on their needs, extensive professional development and support are provided. According to Principal Scotti, "We provide a lot of support. We expect to see the teachers respond to constructive criticism and seek out help when needed. We don't get rid of a teacher after one year—we usually give them another year to improve. It is definitely not sink or swim."

Annie Reynolds adds, "We have the ability and process to remove people. It may sound harsh, but it does leave the teachers here that really want to be teaching here and really believe in the best for the students. We narrow our staff down to the people who are really passionate about it—it creates a completely different feel here."

According to lead teacher Mary Jane Liverpool, "This school offers site-based decision making and flexibility to look at the students in our care and determine what's best for them—what's needed for the future—what's needed right now."

In addition to teacher support and evaluation, the four lead teachers cover myriad administration duties. Don Ormsby clarifies, "Anything that comes up. Distinguished school—we're the writers. Western Association of Schools and Colleges (WASC), charter renewal—we spearhead it. Whatever needs straightening out, we're the go-to people. Yes, it's very demanding, but I'm glad I'm doing it because it's made me a better teacher."

Teachers receive a formal evaluation based on the Four Pillars and teacher professionalism in conducting themselves throughout the school year. Both the principal and lead teacher conduct the conference and sign the evaluation. In addition, the lead teachers are anonymously evaluated by the teachers on their grade level. Lead teachers are evaluated on the following criteria:

- Accessibility (Are they available to you when you need something?)
- Observation process (Provides useful and timely feedback)
- Approachability (Do you feel comfortable going to him/her for advice? Do you feel confident that information and/or advice he/she gives you is reliable?)
- Attitude (Does he/she provide positive leadership in a helpful and supportive manner?)
- Meetings (Are they productive/organized, etc.?)
- Responsive (Follows up on your requests, gets back to you)
- What are other things that your lead teacher can do to help support you better?

These evaluations are submitted to the principal who then discusses them with the lead teacher to identify strengths and areas of improvement.

Also integral to the success of POLAHS's unique leadership structure is the role of the department chair. Department chairs are selected by the principal, based on their mastery of subject matter. Teachers are required to turn in their syllabi and benchmark assessments to the department chairs who, in turn, have the authority and responsibility to hold teachers accountable for the rigor of those content-specific benchmarks and for analyzing student performance on those assessments.

As teachers analyze their assessments using Data Director, the department chairs use these data to ensure that students are receiving quality instruction and that the curriculum is aligned to the standards and concepts required for each class. They are responsible for professional development that is content specific, and also serve as mentors for identified teachers. Department chairs are supported by the lead teachers if there is an issue or concern with a specific teacher.

POLAHS offers a variety of courses to link students' educational options to the Port of Los Angeles. All students take history of the port, which is a graduation requirement. In this course, students visit the port and surrounding maritime community. Other courses and electives include ocean politics, maritime studies, boat operations, logistics, and marine biology. In the boat operations class, students split their time between an actual tugboat and the classroom. They take the boat out one Saturday each month, and have the opportunity to earn Coast Guard certification as deckhands.

To support students' education about the maritime industry, field trips, guest speakers, and internships with organizations are arranged. The Ports of Los Angeles and Long Beach, the U.S. Coast Guard and Customs, the U.S. Corps of Army Engineers, the Marine Exchange of Southern California are a few of the organizations that have provided internships. During the summer institute, new teachers receive maritime-related training to ensure that they are "on board" with the mission and vision of the school.

A variety of programs have been implemented to assist students who are most academically at risk. The Personalized Academic Support Program (PASS) was implemented to work with freshmen and sophomores who do not qualify for an IEP. These students receive individualized academic counseling and tutoring to help them become more proficient academically and organizationally. After-school (seventh-period class two afternoons a week) and weekend study halls specifically target these students. A math intervention program was implemented to assist students who score below basic on the CSTs.

In addition, a math lab provides low-performing students extra support to increase lower-level math skills. With the extra help hired to run the math lab, the student-to-teacher ratio in math classes was lowered to 22:1. Three new classes were added to assist students not prepared for higher-level math and science classes: marine science for students not ready for physics or chemistry, FEM (functions, equations, and modeling) for students between geometry and algebra 2, and basic math that bolsters skills for students not ready for algebra 1 their freshman year.

Every teacher at POLAHS is required to offer at least one hour of tutoring per week. In addition, before finals each semester, teachers stay after school to provide help (so-called cram sessions). After the sessions, a free dinner is provided for the students. Saturday study hall sessions are held throughout the year, and prior to AP exams in the spring, teachers hold Saturday practice test sessions to simulate the testing environment and boost students' confidence.

POLAHS lives up to its vision as a college preparatory high school. Before graduation, students will visit at least a community college, a UC school, a CSU school, and a private college. The school pays for the PSAT for all juniors and any sophomores who wish to take it. A semester-long SAT prep class elective is made available to juniors and seniors. Students are required to write college entrance essays in their junior and senior English classes. Seniors participate in a senior thesis class where they work with a mentor outside of the school to research an issue in their community. The culmination of this project is to present their research to a panel of community members and teachers.

The school has partnered with Los Angeles Harbor College for the past three springs. International business and ethics in engineering have been offered. As Mr. Cross puts it, "We are not just college prep. We have our own graduation requirements, which are beyond the state graduation requirements. We have this pact that they'll be UC ready. We have this philosophy that everybody goes to college."

Technology plays a major role at POLAHS. Every teacher is issued a laptop to take attendance and record grades through the Aeries program. Parents have access to Aeries to check on grades, attendance, and homework. Teachers also use the laptops to create lessons, communicate via their school e-mail accounts, and video stream. Class websites are used to communicate and provide instruction. Students have access to a computer lab and technology center where they learn graphic design, computer science, and 3D animation. Each classroom has a minimum of six computers.

Since POLAHS does not house a traditional library, the school subscribes to EBSCO host, a research database service. Students have access to full text and bibliographic databases for use in their research. Every student is required to write at least one research paper every year.

FUTURE PLANS

At the present time, there are no plans to start another high school, as replicating the success of the unique focus of the maritime curriculum would be difficult. However, POLAHS is in the early exploratory stage of determining the feasibility of opening a feeder middle school. The motivation for starting a middle school is to have the opportunity to better prepare students for the rigors of high school and not have to spend so much time on remediation. In addition, students come to POLAHS without having thought much about college. A POLA middle school could start that mindset earlier.

Plans have been drawn, however, to build a three- or four-story building to provide more classroom space, a second language lab and computer lab, conference rooms, and food services. Still remaining small, the school could offer a few more admission spots to the ever-expanding waiting list.

The school hopes to expand its partnership with Los Angeles Harbor College to include a marine engineering program. The goal is to provide the school with three tracks for students in the maritime studies program that lead to separate internships: logistics, politics, and engineering. These three tracks will ultimately give students entrée to the California Maritime Academy and other similar programs.

CONCLUSIONS

In 2005 the San Pedro Chamber of Commerce dreamed of a school that would be an integral part of the downtown San Pedro community and a partner with the Port of Los Angeles. The goal was to create positive and mutually beneficial relationships with neighboring businesses, public agencies, and community organizations. It is clear that the Port of Los Angeles High School has lived up to that dream. The innovative Maritime Studies and International Business focus continues to expand. The Port of Los Angeles provides funds for professional development, guest speakers, and police services.

The San Pedro Chamber of Commerce uses POLAHS student volunteers for community events, and sponsors groups of students to chamber-sponsored conferences and educational events. There are paid and unpaid internships, volunteer and job-shadowing opportunities with the Port of Los Angeles and other San Pedro businesses.

The unique lead teacher program provides a high level of support and accountability for all teachers to hold high expectations for students both academically and behaviorally. This program was instrumental in the school becoming a Distinguished School in 2011.

The school is immaculate and welcoming. There is a business-like atmosphere, with rooms that are colorful and inviting and that reflect the professional demeanor expected from all students. When teachers dismiss students from class, there are no bells sounded. According to James Cross, "Everybody enjoys being here; it's really been wonderful. I probably spend $30,000 or more on paint—50 percent of the school is painted every summer just so it looks pristine all the time. We spend a lot of money on buffing floors and patching holes. Does it make the difference? I can't quantify it. We treat kids as adults. We wear suits every day. It's a million little things. It's the collective. You can't take one piece out—it's a great atmosphere."

KEY ELEMENTS

- The partnership with the Port of Los Angeles provides students the opportunity to study and work in, and ultimately more fully understand and embrace, their community.
- Lead teachers and department chairs comprise a unique governance structure to ensure the highest-quality instruction for students and support for teachers.
- PASS, tutoring, and "cram sessions" provide students extra support.

Part IV

CHARTER SPAN SCHOOLS

CHAPTER 12

Camino Nuevo Charter Academy
Los Angeles, California

INTRODUCTION

Just west of downtown, on a side street bordering busy Wilshire Boulevard, sits Camino Nuevo Charter Academy Burlington K–8 Campus, a model for transformational change taking on one of the most challenging neighborhoods Los Angeles has to offer. The MacArthur Park area, with its open grass space and large lake, began as a vacation destination in the 1890s, known then as the "Champs-Élysées of L.A." The former luxury hotels surrounding the park have since been converted to apartments, providing dilapidated housing for legions of immigrants from Mexico and Central America hoping to find a better life for themselves and their children.

As often happens in large cities, the MacArthur Park area became poor, overpopulated, and underserved, falling prey to gangs, drugs, and crime by the 1980s. It is against this backdrop that the story of Camino Nuevo Charter Academy emerges and why this school sees itself as more than just a place to teach children reading, writing, and arithmetic.

Unlike many charter schools in Los Angeles, Camino Nuevo is one that was founded by and for the community. Philip Lance, an Episcopal minister working with families in the area, realized that there was a need for community-based leadership and founded the nonprofit Pueblo Nuevo. According to Camino Nuevo's principal, Sean Holiday, "What they saw was the real need for a school," so they converted a crumbling strip mall into a school in 2000. "The roots are in the community, the roots are with the parents, with the families, and with the people who gave their lives to this community," continued Holiday.

"This is what makes Camino Nuevo so different; it came from the community based on a real need."

Today the school is housed in colorful buildings overlooking a central playground and covered eating area. The excitement of the students and the bright and positive atmosphere created by caring adults is in direct contrast to the surrounding neighborhood.

The school's mission is to educate students in a college preparatory program to be literate, critical thinkers, and independent problem solvers who are agents of social justice with sensitivity toward the world around them. Former principal Atyani Howard noted that "what we want to see in every classroom is excellent instruction, authentic literacy, critical thinking, and high levels of engagement—engagement coming from students and teachers."

The path that Holiday himself took to become principal began with a Teach for America assignment here, then a move to assistant principal, and then principal. His longevity at this campus has helped him build the relationships and trust that are essential for a successful administrator.

"I have many people on my leadership team: an assistant principal, a dean of culture, an operations coordinator, a director of student and family services," he said. He believes that living the mission of the school means having a team that tries to be as nonhierarchical as possible. The school has an instructional cadre where teachers have a strong voice in making decisions about curriculum and instruction. Another factor that sets Camino Nuevo apart from other charters is its Camino Nuevo Teachers Association, a teachers' union that participates in decision making as well.

The seven schools within the Camino Nuevo Charter organization are governed by a board of directors and guided by the Home Support Office, which enables each school to have the autonomy it needs to experiment. This autonomy affords each school the ability to try new things while working within a framework to which they are all committed.

Camino Nuevo, like most charter schools, runs on data. Currently student enrollment is around 563 students in kindergarten through eighth grade, made up of 98 percent Hispanic, 98 percent Socioeconomically Disadvantaged, 65 percent ELs, 10 percent SWDs, and 35 percent Reclassified Fluent English Proficient.

Data Implications

Year	Enrollment	% AI	Ethnicity			
			% Asian/Filipino/ Pacific Islander	% Black	% Hispanic	% White
2012–13	563	0.2	0	0.4	98.0	0.2
2011–12	567	0.2	0.2	0.5	98.1	0.2
2010–11	529	0.2	0.2	0.6	98.5	0

Year	% Socioeconomic	% English Learners	% Students w/ Disabilities
2012–13	98.2	64.8	9.8
2011–12	98.9	63.3	10.7
2010–11	99.1	64.3	9.9

Year	API	% AYP—English Lang Arts*	% Mathematics*
2012–13	821	51.1	70.5
2011–12	824	56.0	67.4
2010–11	838	54.4	77.6

* = Percent at/above Proficient

While most of their students come from the surrounding area, many travel from as far as Covina, Lancaster, and South Los Angeles to attend school. "We have a large wait list," said Holiday. "We hold a public lottery in February. In our kinder class, we have sixty-six seats and we could probably fill that three times."

Their API moved from 718 in 2007 to 821 by 2013, and the school earned an API similar schools rank of ten and a statewide rank of six. In that same year, Camino Nuevo surpassed the local LAUSD schools their students would attend like Esperanza Elementary at 675 and Berendo Middle School at 739.

On the 2013 California Standards Tests, grades two through eight averaged 51 percent proficient/advanced in English language arts and 71 percent in math. Proficient/advanced scores for the school averaged 72 percent in algebra, 100 percent in geometry, and 78 percent in science. This growth and achievement has earned them the California Association of Bilingual Education Seal of Excellence Award, the California Title I Academic Achievement Award, and the California Distinguished Elementary School Award, as well as a six-year accreditation by the Western Association of Schools and Colleges.

Holiday is definitely the team leader when it comes to data. He has a ready knowledge of the school's demographics and achievement and uses that information to make sound decisions. "We use our data to decide professional development activities. For example, last year we had challenges with student behavior so we focused on school culture during professional development," he stated.

Leadership also uses the teacher survey and focus groups. "We are observing the school and classrooms all the time so we have data there," according to Holiday. The school decided to focus on school culture, English language development and phonics, the Common Core standards, and differentiated approaches in response to the data they gathered. The professional-development calendar is created in May for the following school year and the theme "Teach to Reach" helps teachers continue to differentiate instruction while promoting a positive school culture.

Additionally Camino Nuevo gathers student data through regularly scheduled formative assessments. These benchmarks are given in October, January, and March or April and are aligned to standards, with the results scanned into Data Director.

"Teachers analyze their own data with their team," said Holiday. "Then I meet with each team to look at trends across the grade level. Then I meet with each individual teacher to identify trends in their classroom, a practice we do three times a year." These benchmarks, according to Holiday, are crucial to his teachers monitoring student progress and adjusting instruction.

The school works to involve parents by teaching them how to read with their children, how to write with them, and how to do Singapore Math. "When you're buying bananas at the store," explained Holiday, "you might want six bananas and have three in your hand—how many more do I need?" This type of direct approach to engaging parents at an easily accessible level puts the focus on the skill and not on the percentage correct on an exam.

SUCCESS FACTORS

The success Camino Nuevo has enjoyed springs from the dedicated people who founded it and the current staff of administrators, teachers, and others who work with a single purpose, to provide the best possible education for their students.

"Teaching is first," said Holiday when asked why his school is a model for success. The selection of teachers is a process that works to find people who have demonstrated an alignment with the vision and mission of the school. "We post jobs online," said Holiday. "We recruit through networks like Loyola Marymount University, UCLA, and Teach for America."

The process includes a phone screening, an interview, a demonstration lesson, a debrief, a data analysis, writing exercises, self-reflection exercises, and an interview with the team the candidate would be working with. "The mission and vision is something we really interview for; it's the first fourteen questions of the interview process. The reason we have so many steps," continued Holiday, "is that we know the biggest lever of change is the teacher, so we work hard to recruit teachers who are exceptional."

Occasionally, teachers struggle in this challenging environment. "Every teacher has a coach," said Holiday. "I coach teachers in grades three, four, six, seven, and eight. My AP coaches kindergarten, one, two, and five. That means I'm observing them regularly, meeting with them about once every two weeks, debriefing observations, providing support; we really know our teachers' classrooms."

These site administrators demonstrate lessons, videotape lessons, have teachers observe other teachers, call in support from the Camino Nuevo home office or other groups, in addition to its professional development program—in short, the school offers its teachers every opportunity for growth.

Much of what is taught is teacher created and standards based; the school has chosen not to use prewritten, scripted reading programs like Open Court or Treasures. Instead, it embraces a balanced literacy approach that focuses on the Four Blocks of Literacy framework within a bilingual program.

"Our bilingual program runs kindergarten through fifth starting with 80 percent Spanish in kindergarten, moving to 70 percent English by fifth grade and all English in the middle school grades," stated Holiday. "Our bilingual program is an act of social justice. We ensure that our students value their home language and their communities."

The school's Singapore Conceptual Math K–5 program moves from the concrete to the pictorial to the abstract, and the College Preparatory Math program is text heavy and builds upon the work done in the elementary grades. The school's systematic English language development utilizes explicit teaching for high levels of speaking. Students have access to art, drama, dance, and music throughout their time at the school, though not all at the same time.

Additionally, middle school students get a half-hour reading block every day based on their area of need in accordance with the Teachers College Reading and Writing program from Columbia University. "We have a reading class for students who need help in summarizing, inferential comprehension, a motivation class, book-groups class—students are really able to have a reading class based on their area of need and they rotate throughout the year," explained Holiday. "They have electives based on what they need like math intervention or English Language Development (ELD); they also have access to classes like student council, peer counseling, drama, art, and cross training. These electives change based on data and student desire."

Camino Nuevo operates on an extended school year, providing 195 instructional days from August to June and a school day that starts at 8:00 a.m. and runs to 3:00 p.m. for the elementary grades and 3:15 p.m. for the middle school. The teachers have two hours of professional development each week, and twice a month the staff meets after school, with much of the time spent in teacher teams.

The school strongly emphasizes authentic learning and there is very little explicit test prep. "Students are reading books and writing essays and playing with manipulatives, and really learning what it is to do math, what it is to write an essay," said Holiday. "The biggest area for growth is reaching the kids that are the hardest to reach, kids that are not special-education students but still really struggle and need plenty of support. That is why we brought on some instructional teachers' assistants who are going to target those kids who need a little push."

The school uses an inclusion model, where resource students get the extra support they need from resource teachers within their classrooms. The differentiation extends to electives like geometry and reading blocks, where students read novels and newspapers like the *Wall Street Journal* to challenge the gifted and high achieving.

To fulfill the mission of the school, and especially to underscore the social justice element, Camino Nuevo works hard to provide students the enrichment that other more affluent communities take for granted. "Giving students opportunities to go to places like Washington, D.C., Catalina, and Astro Camp in San Francisco, and to go on hikes and really see the world as theirs—that's an act of social justice," commented Holiday. "Literacy—that's an act of social justice. These are all ways that our vision and mission come alive."

The school has many community partners to help it realize its goals, including counseling provided by the Los Angeles Child Development Center, interns from USC, and Didi Hirsch Mental Health Services. The Los Angeles Philharmonic brings music education to the school, P.S. Arts gives art and theater instruction, and Everybody Dance teaches dance and movement. The long-standing roots in the community and the many community partners gathered by the Camino Nuevo organization have contributed to creating the best possible support for this successful school.

Another essential element that makes Camino Nuevo stand out is its commitment to and from its parents. The school's philosophy is that parent participation is not a one-shot volunteer opportunity or a string of disconnected activities. To reach this objective, the school has built an infrastructure around parents as partners. The evidence of this partnership is everywhere on campus, with parents warmly greeted in their home language when they enter the main office or walk the halls.

Parents are free to visit the campus and actively participate in the many workshops and activities the school has to offer them. At a recent parent-appreciation meeting, the room was packed with over 120 parents, most of them receiving honors for the many volunteer hours they have devoted to the school. Camino Nuevo asks for fifteen hours a year, but Holiday conferred awards to many parents with 50 to over 250 hours served last year.

"We provide workshops on college planning, family planning, résumé building, interview skills, book clubs, and how to discipline with love—workshops every day," said Holiday. He feels that these tools empower parents, especially those from traumatized communities. The core values the parent workshops support are *P*ersistence, *O*wnership, *D*esire, *E*mpowerment, and *R*espect: PODER.

"These are all things we try to live through our actions," said Holiday. "We try to make the connection a little clearer by saying, 'We're having this workshop on X and X is connected to PODER because . . .'" Parents also have leadership opportunities on their School Site Council and English Language Advisory Council (ELAC), and feel comfortable discussing their concerns with the principal whose open-door policy and visibility around the campus make him easily accessible to everyone.

The school holds Back-to-School Night, Family Math Night, and Books-in-Pajamas Night to help connect families with the academic nature of the school. It also organizes school-wide socials, barbecues, and school dances as often as possible. This year the school will feature a poetry slam, giving students the opportunity to share their creative talents with their parents and their peers. These activities make Camino Nuevo a community center, a place where parents as well as students can find support in reaching their goals.

FUTURE PLANS

Keeping this school operating smoothly and effectively at its current level is an ambitious undertaking, with the many variables and outside influences that affect student achievement. Camino Nuevo's goals for its future go beyond maintaining the success it has had. "Our vision for this school is to create a trauma-sensitive environment that supports all of our students," stated Holiday. We need to figure out how to push our school to improve academic performance. We are not getting to every kid—how do we push every kid? We need to do a better job of that."

It is precisely this unblinking honesty and refusal to be complacent that sets Camino Nuevo apart. Where others might be happy with the tremendous strides this school has made in challenging conditions, the staff, parents, and community will continue to exhaust every avenue to create and support excellence, and in so doing make a significant difference in the lives of each student and, hopefully, in this city.

CONCLUSIONS

Camino Nuevo's authentic success truly stems from its grassroots inception and the dedication the school community has to living up to the promise of the school's mission. While many campuses are a place of work, this campus is a place of optimism. With the ideal of social justice and the civil right of each student to have the best possible education as its guiding principles, this school moves ahead by assessing progress and carefully planning to support student learning.

Pueblo Nuevo has allowed this school and the other charters under its purview to develop and grow, encouraging and valuing the contribution of teachers, staff, and parents in support of student progress.

KEY ELEMENTS

- A mission that is lived each day at the school by all stakeholders; the perception that literacy is a civil right and that creating literate, well-educated students is an act of social justice.
- A tangible response to a traumatized student and family population through targeted parent classes and workshops, and student and family counseling.
- The continuity of leadership, where teachers are supported and valued as leaders and promotion is often from within the organization.
- Data-driven decision making that includes all stakeholders.
- Careful and inclusive planning for instruction and professional development.
- Purposeful activities, such as field trips, social activities for students and families, and school activities to help close the gap between students of poverty and those of affluence.

CHAPTER 13

Gabriella Charter School
Los Angeles, California

INTRODUCTION

When in 1999 a tragic accident took the life of thirteen-year-old Gabriella Axelrad, her mother, Liza Bercovici, determined that her daughter would not be forgotten. She wanted to honor and preserve her daughter's memory and bring something good out of it. Gabriella loved to dance, and wanted to become a teacher. Although having no personal experience in either dance or education, Ms. Bercovici gave up her law practice in order to create the Gabriella Axelrad Foundation to bring dance education to inner-city children.

In May of 2000 the Everybody Dance! program was formed to offer free and low-cost weekly ballet, tap, jazz, hip hop, and modern dance classes to children who would otherwise not have access to them. The original location was a low-income-housing building across from MacArthur Park near downtown Los Angeles. Ms. Bercovici became an accomplished fund-raiser, and the nonprofit organization soon was able to serve more than the thirty-five original students. In fact, it has grown to serve more than a thousand children with over three thousand on the waiting list.

During this time, the Camino Nuevo Charter School was also located in the same building. The foundation began offering dance classes to that school's students after school. Parents and teachers began to notice how the very high expectations held for students in the dance program were motivating and benefiting all students but especially the second-language learners. They were asking, "Please can you do more?" Since there were so many positive outcomes for students with after-school dance lessons, the question became: What could be accomplished if there were a school where students could dance every day?

In 2005 Gabriella Charter School (GCS) opened in the same location with five classes: two kindergarten classes and one first-, second-, and third-grade class. Principal Lisa Rooney was one of the founding teachers. She was looking for a place where "everybody really truly believes that all students should and can succeed at high levels and where parent participation is not only encouraged, but it's the benchmark that's expected."

Liza Bercovici believed that schools have the right to define their own mission and vision, and staffed the school with Teach for America teachers who had at least two years of experience. In addition, the first principal, Susan Gurman, was a Teach for America teacher with more than twenty years of experience. They knew that teachers liked to work in a high-performing environment and that it wouldn't be hard to attract high-performing teachers because they would want to work with other high-performing colleagues where they felt challenged and stimulated. They put the staff together and gave them the freedom to create the vision.

As first-grade teacher Nicolette Zimmerman tells it, "I'm not just working harder but better than I've ever worked before. The tone of the school is that we are here to perform at our best and we will do anything we have to succeed. I like performing at this level—I'm surrounded by others performing at this level who are just as motivated as I am."

Ms. Bercovici says, "Fired up young teachers should be given the ability to craft the school—and they did. If Susan and I get credit, it's for stepping back and letting go." In its second year of operation, *Los Angeles* magazine described GCS as "one of sixty great elementary schools you should know about." In addition to numerous awards for excellence, GCS has been identified as a Title I Academic Achievement Award recipient.

In 2008 GCS colocated with a LAUSD school, Logan Street Elementary School in Echo Park. In 2009 sixth grade was added, in 2010, seventh grade, and in 2011, eighth grade. The decision to add the middle school came because of pressure from parents looking for alternatives to their lack of acceptable middle school options. Originally the plan was to have two separate schools, an elementary school and a middle school. However, at that time LAUSD mandated that the elementary students could not automatically matriculate to the middle school. Since this was the impetus for adding the middle school, the decision was made to make GCS a kindergarten through eighth grade school to guarantee continuous enrollment.

School enrollment is determined by a random public lottery. Preference is given to students who live within the LAUSD attendance boundaries, to the siblings of students already attending GCS, and to children of school employees. While keeping class sizes small has benefited students, it has also created disappointed families who are not selected in the lottery. There is always a long waiting list of hopeful applicants.

The current school enrollment at Gabriella is 433, having grown from sixty when the school opened its doors in 2005. Of those students, 86 percent are Hispanic, 7 percent are Asian/Filipino/Pacific Islander, 3 percent African American, and 4 percent White. Approximately 89 percent of the students qualify for the Free and Reduced-Price Lunch Program (Socioeconomically Disadvantaged), 30 percent are ELs, and 14 percent are SWDs.

Data Implications

Year	Enrollment	% AI	% Asian/Filipino/ Pacific Islander	% Black	% Hispanic	% White
			Ethnicity			
2012–13	433	0	6.7	2.8	86.1	3.9
2011–12	426	0.2	6.6	3.5	84.3	4.0
2010–11	354	0	8.2	4.2	83.3	4.0

Year	% Socioeconomic	% English Learners	% Students w/ Disabilities
2012–13	88.7	29.8	14.4
2011–12	89.9	37.8	14.0
2010–11	31.9	44.9	13.3

Year	API	% AYP—English Lang Arts*	% Mathematics*
2012–13	892	71.8	81.2
2011–12	894	76.8	79.6
2010–11	875	62.4	82.0

* = Percent at/above Proficient

In its nine years of operation, the API has risen from 854 to 894—a significant achievement, considering the fact that these gains were made in spite of adding enrollment and adding the middle school scores for the sixth and seventh grades. In the 2009/2010 school year, the EL subgroup failed to make its Annual Measurable Objective (AMO) for English language arts (ELA). However, in the next year, GCS met seventeen of seventeen AMOs through Safe Harbor by showing progress in moving students scoring at the below-proficient level to the proficient level.

Gabriella is especially proud of its CST scores in mathematics. For example, in fourth grade, the percentages of students advanced and proficient in mathematics were 92 percent (2009), 90 percent (2010), and 91 percent (2011). In 2011 only six students were basic, two were below basic, and none were far below basic.

While celebrating their excellent mathematics scores, the administrators and teachers recognize that their ELA scores, although good, are not as strong. Again using fourth grade as an example, the percentages of students advanced and proficient in ELA were 70 percent (2009), 76 percent (2010), and 57 percent (2011). An examination of these data became the impetus for providing more professional development in ELA.

SUCCESS FACTORS

GCS is a dance-themed school that provides one hour of dance instruction for every student every day. The school day is longer to accommodate this program so that all other curricular areas are not neglected. In the dance program very high expectations are held for students. The dance instructors are very strict and expect students to take their instruction seriously. Students are expected to come on time; they are expected to come fully dressed. If they are not, they do not participate. Then they will watch and do a reflection so that they will be ready to participate fully next time. As students work with each other as a group to music, they not only get exercise and the kinesthetic experience, but have the opportunity to be creative as well.

Dance is infused into the standards-based curriculum. The dance teachers collaborate closely with the homeroom teachers and develop dance lessons that correlate to the standards being taught in the classroom. For example, students in second grade are taught movements to help them internalize telling time. Gestures used to illustrate vocabulary words are e-mailed to the dance teachers so that they can reinforce the classroom concepts in the dance studio. To support third-grade science instruction, students learn a dance about crayfish, and a dance about the states of matter.

It is believed that the discipline, creativity, and cognitive aspects of dance motivate students to be more active learners academically. Teachers believe that when students are asked to do things that no one knows how to do, they see that there are no failures in dance if they persevere and do their best. Teachers say that no matter how hard something is, students will always try and give it 100 percent. This carries over to their classrooms where they are not afraid to stand up and give an answer. They know that if they get it wrong, no one is going to make fun of them.

In the discipline of dance, teamwork is valued. Students learn early on that they cannot waste other students' time, and that they will not be allowed to ruin a performance by exhibiting poor behavior that pulls the audience's attention from the dance. Everyone must do their part in the choreography to have a successful outcome; the same holds true for projects in their classrooms.

Students have choreography once a week where it brings everything together—it is the application of their work in dance. Principal Lisa Rooney likens it to the writing process. The students brainstorm and think of ideas activating prior knowledge from their other classrooms. Then the dance teachers help them take ideas from what they're learning in their classroom and teach the students how to choreograph and how to write it out—how to make dance movement sentences that are ultimately revised, edited, and published as a performance.

No matter whom you ask, dance is not the answer to the question, "What makes Gabriella so successful?" To be sure it is a very important factor. However, the first answer from Founder Bercovici, Principal Rooney, and the teachers is that success comes from extremely high expectations for both academics and behavior. The combination of very clear expectations of what is expected, combined with support and rewards for excelling, build the culture of the school; there is also a very clear message of what will not be tolerated. These high expectations are held for everyone—students, teachers, administration, and parents. The standards are high, but reachable.

Everyone at the school supports these high expectations. During standardized testing last spring, everyone from the executive director to the classified staff was videotaped encouraging the students. The assistant custodian, who doesn't speak English, said in Spanish, "I want you guys to do well. Everybody needs to be here and not miss a day of testing." The students got the sense of doing well for their community. Much as when children want to please their parents because they matter so much to them, GCS is their extended family and the students have a very strong sense of responsibility. Their family members are all rooting for them to do well on the test so they get the message that they must show up and do their best. It is a nonnegotiable.

The high expectations are operationalized though consistent standards enforced by all staff. Starting in kindergarten, students know what's expected of them, and that spirals up through the grades. There are no big changes, or surprises. They know that there's a consistent expectation for behavior and academics and all of it is known from the very beginning. This ensures that students don't have to waste time relearning things, and they don't have to learn new ways of doing things.

Certain protocols, such as working in collaborative groups, meeting with writing partners, and literature circle work, are learned early. This allows time to be used productively so that teachers can take students deeper into the curriculum. Behavior protocols are also learned early. SLANT starts in kindergarten and is utilized in every grade. SLANT is the acronym for S=Sit up; L=Listen; A=Ask and Answer; N=Nod for understanding; and T=Track the Speaker. When students hear "SLANT," they know what is expected.

The way teachers interact with students is positive but no-nonsense. Project-based constructivism is not the basis of instructional practice at GCS although there are many projects and products that culminate units of study. Teachers provide direct instruction by modeling concepts, and then giving students a great deal of guided practice before having them work independently.

An essential component is feedback. Students are given immediate constructive feedback through teacher conferences, rubric comments, and peer critical friends. From a young age they receive feedback and learn that it is not criticism. They get that in dance every day when they are standing in front of a mirror and hearing their classmates say, "When you did this it made it hard for us to learn" or "Your lines were not straight and my attention was drawn to you, so let's work on that." This is the norm for them. Students want to hear more than compliments—they know that feedback helps them improve.

The curriculum at GCS is rigorous and standards based but is adapted to varying skill and ability levels and learning styles. There is no separate curriculum for ELs, special-education students who are fully included, or gifted students. Extensive formative and summative assessments provide teachers with the necessary information to challenge all of their students at their appropriate level. Additionally, because there are two teachers at each grade level who team teach, both teachers know all the students well. One teacher teaches ELA and social studies, while the other team member teaches mathematics and science. During dance each day, the two teachers are released to meet and review their students' progress, plan curriculum, and discuss in depth their students' strengths and weaknesses.

In addition to grade-level teams, teachers are in curricular pods. The kindergarten through second-grade teachers work together; the third- through fifth-grade ELA teachers and third- through fifth-grade math/science teachers work together. Professional-development time is devoted to the pods so that teachers can set their own goals and decide what to work on—all based on student work. Since Gabriella's math scores are high (nearly 80 percent advanced and proficient), a focus for grades three through five in professional development is in ELA—specifically how to help math/science teachers support literacy and teach reading and writing in their content.

The research is clear that the most important factor in any child's education is the effectiveness of the teachers and administration. Gabriella benefited from Liza Bercovici hiring the right people. As Lisa Rooney puts it, "One of her big strengths in addition to being the person who never takes no for an answer, is making sure that the right people are hired. She has a knack for it." The hiring process is rigorous and has been refined over the years. A great deal of time was spent determining the qualities desired in the ideal teacher and identifying the indicators of those qualities.

The process starts with an application with essay questions. If candidates demonstrate strong writing and communication skills, and a relentless focus on student outcomes, they are invited to present a demonstration lesson. In the debriefing following the lesson, the team looks for specific points. Since expectations for student engagement and behavior are high, the candidates' reflection on how the lesson went in those areas is very revealing as to how the candidate will fit into the Gabriella culture. The last step is a structured interview.

A recent addition to the Gabriella staff, second-grade teacher Julie Halton recalls the process being rigorous with three hours for the interview, a demo lesson, a phone interview, a meeting with administration and teachers, and presentation of a portfolio. She agrees with the importance of handpicking the teachers, "Everyone here wants to be here. My students will have phenomenal teachers from kindergarten to eighth grade—strong teachers all the way through."

The teachers have high praise for their principal with whom they meet for an hour every other week. This meeting can focus on whatever the teacher needs. It can be about students, assessment, curriculum, report cards, what's working, what's not working—she is seen as a real resource and support. Ms. Bercovici also has high praise for her administrative and teaching staff and acknowledges the benefits of GCS not being unionized. "If someone is not meeting our standard, they're just not invited back the following year. Yes, there is a process for support—we don't want turnover. We don't want to lose great people."

Parent involvement is very important; there are parents at the gate, serving lunch, and in the classrooms. Parents know that they are wanted and needed as partners at GCS. Gabriella has a really clear list of expectations for parents. Parents do sign the homework logs; they do sign up for service hours; they do show up for parent-teacher conferences. Parents do respond to teacher notes and correspondence and inquiries. Everyone internalizes what's expected and the consequence is that students do well.

Although the law states parents cannot be required to participate, the expectation is clear. They are to volunteer fifteen hours of service a year with five more for each additional child (a maximum of twenty-five hours). Parents are asked to serve at least two meals a year as well as come to Saturday workdays. They help clean during the summer and inventory supplies. Each quarter teachers hold a classroom meeting for parents to help them help their students at home. For example, the first-grade team modeled how to ask questions when parents are reading with their children. They did a mini-lesson with all the students in the front, and then gave parents feedback when they were practicing with their children.

FUTURE PLANS

According to Liza Bercovici, "I'm very proud of everything we've achieved, but I don't think that we should rest on our laurels either. I think we need to keep driving forward in making sure that our kids will have the same opportunities as anybody else graduating from public school anywhere in the world. That should be, in my opinion, our standard." Opening other GCS sites is being considered.

GCS is helping eighth-grade parents navigate the process of selecting a high school for their students. They work with parents to try to get private-school scholarships for their students. Some students will go to the LAUSD Performing Arts High School and others will go to their neighborhood high school. All eighth-grade parents were invited to school to get e-mail accounts so that they could complete the LAUSD Choices brochure online to start the process of getting points for selection into the district's magnet program. Opening a Gabriella High School is under consideration.

CONCLUSIONS

Fourth-grade teachers Jamie Campbell and Michelle Alpert sum it up. They say, "Students arrive at GCS every day with smiling faces with all of their homework done. It shows that it doesn't really matter where you come from if you work hard and your parents are committed.

These students are motivated and like to work together. Everything is here—we haven't taken out social studies and science. They get music and art in addition to dance."

A visit to Gabriella validates that a culture of high expectations is the norm. Students are smiling as they come through the gate in the morning, and those smiles stay with them all day. In classrooms students are fully engaged while being respectful and responsive to the slightest cue to modify behavior. On the playground, students line up quickly and quietly. Teachers are also fully engaged, providing instruction in full group, small groups, and one-on-one conferences. They meet with their team partner to better meet the needs of their students. Expectations are high for everyone, but reachable by all.

A little first-grade student waiting to be picked up because she had pink eye made the specialness of Gabriella Charter School very clear. When asked what she liked best about her school, instead of talking about dance she said, "We get to do poetry!" She then talked about how she loved math and explained in great detail how to determine greater than and less than. She demonstrated the movements she had learned to help reinforce the concepts and then very adeptly wrote some number sentences down using the correct symbols. She clearly did not want to go home and miss one minute of the GCS experience.

KEY ELEMENTS

- The goal of GCS is to strengthen student success with academics and behavior through the use of dance; it is not to turn out good dancers.
- Dance instruction allows grade-level teachers to meet on a daily basis to review their students' progress, and plan instruction based on their students' specific needs.
- A rigorous hiring process ensures that teachers are held to the highest standards of the GCS culture of high expectations for student success.
- Parent participation is a critical component of the GCS success story.

CHAPTER 14

Larchmont Charter School
Los Angeles, California

INTRODUCTION

Parents in the greater Hollywood/Hancock Park area held some basic assumptions about the public schools in their neighborhood: Public schools are not sufficiently high performing; public schools are not diverse—they don't represent the full diversity of the community; and they were not engaging the best education practices, i.e., constructivist pedagogy. These parents banded together to create an independent public charter school in their community that was open to all, diverse, and informed by constructivism. That was the genesis, grounded both in their unique perspective and their ambition that became Larchmont Charter School in 2005.

Students from anywhere in California are admitted by annual lottery with priority given to those who live within LAUSD boundaries; neighborhood kids no longer have priority. Though the neighborhood surrounding the campus is very diverse, neighborhood public school populations do not reflect this diversity. According to Executive Director Brian Johnson, there is a reason for that. He explains that in public education in Los Angeles, students are being underserved when compared to their peers in other large urban school districts.

This shortfall breaks down for two groups of kids differently. In one group, students are suffering from the achievement gap; they are not achieving on par with their peers in high-income communities. In the second group families are opting out of public schools. One out of four white families, one out of five Asian families, and one out of eight African American families in Los Angeles are not sending their kids to public schools. The result is that traditional public schools do not fully represent the diversity of the community in diverse neighborhoods. Groups are self-segregating into different schools.

The founding parents believed that there is a cycle of segregation being reinforced by not having a lot of schools that have kids from all backgrounds together. So they said, "Wouldn't it be powerful if we could demonstrate that children representing all backgrounds could come together from the full range of the socioeconomic sector, from the children of Oscar and Emmy nominees and network presidents going to school with first-generation Americans whose parents are yet to speak English. This would really reflect the full dynamic of diversity of LA."

Pairing this belief with an education philosophy that's informed by constructivism and project-based learning could demonstrate to the broader community that if things are done differently, the entire community could be pulled back to our public schools.

At Larchmont there are three classes at every grade level; kindergarten and first grade are taught together so that there are six kindergarten-first grade classes, each supported by a fully credentialed teacher, and its own teacher assistant. Also, there are six second-third grade classes, taught by six teachers and supported by four teacher assistants.

This grade-level configuration has many advantages. There is a great deal of collaboration between the six teachers in each team. There are flexible reading and math groups even at this level so that teachers are working with developmentally and academically homogenous as well as heterogeneous groups. With such a diverse group of students from different backgrounds, different learning styles, and twelve different languages, it has worked well to have the split grades.

In the upper grades, teachers team teach utilizing a block schedule. All teachers teach English language arts to their own classes and then team for math, science, and social studies, and provide students with opportunities for a great deal of integration between subject areas. There are two teacher assistants for fourth grade and two for fifth grade.

The campus is currently housed in space leased from the Hollygrove Children and Family Services in Hollywood. Originally a K–2 school, it is now a K–5 at that site, and has a 6–8 middle school at the Immanuel Presbyterian Church. Another K–8 Larchmont school, Larch-

Data Implications

Year	Enrollment	% AI	% Asian/Filipino/ Pacific Islander	% Black	% Hispanic	% White
			Ethnicity			
2012–13	679	0.4	22.1	8.2	22.7	46.1
2011–12	606	0.5	20.5	8.4	20.0	50.7
2010–11	492	0.6	19.1	8.1	17.3	53.7

Year	% Socioeconomic	% English Learners	% Students w/ Disabilities
2012–13	39.2	4.7	11.2
2011–12	41.7	3.1	12.3
2010–11	26.4		13.6

Year	API	% AYP—English Lang Arts*	% Mathematics*
2012–13	909	81.2	76.5
2011–12	923	84.7	78.5
2010–11	931	83.8	85.8

* = Percent at/above Proficient

mont Charter West Hollywood, was founded in 2008. As enrollment at the Hollygrove site has grown, classroom space has become severely limited. Classes are currently held in rooms that were originally small four-bed dorm rooms in an orphanage.

The current enrollment at Larchmont is 679. The ethnic breakdown is 46 percent White, 22 percent Asian, 23 percent Hispanic, and 8 percent African American. The data demonstrate a trend of reducing the number of White students (60.2 percent in 2008/2009 to 46.1 percent in 2012/2013). There is a concomitant increase in other ethnicities over the same time period, which supports the primary mission of diversity of the school. Approximately 39 percent of the students are on the Free and Reduced-Price Lunch program (Socioeconomically Disadvantaged), 5 percent are ELs, and 11 percent are SWDs.

The school's API has gone up 55 points from Larchmont's inception (854 in 2006) to the present (909 in 2013). In spite of this excellent API score, the Hispanic subgroup had difficulty meeting their AMOs for ELA and mathematics. However, they were able to meet their AMOs through the alternative method of Safe Harbor.

The Larchmont philosophy revolves around a constant and thorough examination of the data to make decisions that will provide success for all students. As Director Brian Johnson notes, there are schools "hitting it out of the park" with "drill and kill" and others "with a constructivism side I call creative care—where students do deep thinking and feel good about themselves." But for Larchmont, he feels, "When you work in a really diverse setting, our belief is that we've got to do both things very well. So we've got to have an outcomes focus, so we set academic goals and benchmarks and assess our kids to check on how they're doing, and we do this in a constructivist, project-based thematic learning environment."

SUCCESS FACTORS

Larchmont's project-based constructivist philosophy supports the view that every child has different strengths, talents, and assets that they bring to bear, and each child learns differently. With a diverse population of students, programs and structures must serve each student or group of students differently, while holding the same expectations for all. To support this focus, class sizes are kept small (22:1 in the kindergarten through fourth grade classes, and 23:1 in grade five).

To differentiate for these students, the majority of the school's budget is allocated for personnel. There are seventeen teaching assistants, three of whom are fully credentialed, who work with small groups of students to reinforce concepts, support the intervention program, and work with special-education students.

There is not a set curriculum or set of resources that is the answer. As teacher Nora Robinson puts it, "We're designing curriculum. It's not like you can walk in when the kids walk in and flip to page seventeen and just read the Open Court lesson; there's so much that has to go into it beyond just the time you spend with the kids."

Fourth-grade teacher Amanda Koniezny points out that "there are no constructivist books at Barnes and Noble." Teachers read research and then implement it. If it doesn't work, they evaluate and reflect and try something else. Teachers realize that they do not have all the answers and work together to find ways to reach every student.

Rachel Green says, "I came here because I wasn't able to teach the way I passionately believed I should be teaching for the people in my room. When you sign on here, you're not signing on to follow a teachers' manual, not signing on to go home at 3:00 p.m. Teachers who don't share the vision are not asked back and we're all OK with that."

It is that combination of high expectations and outcomes-focused education with a constructivist education philosophy that is creating success for Larchmont students. In addition to standardized tests, academic goals and benchmarks are set, and students are assessed regularly to check on how they're doing. Rubrics, demonstrations of learning, and written projects are just a few of the ways that students' progress is monitored.

Data are constantly examined to determine if certain subsets are progressing. As Brian Johnson says, "As I like to remind our school leaders, data doesn't give you the answers, it just tells you the right questions to ask. The answers still live with our experts, our teachers, and our principals." Collaboratively working with the data, and then analyzing it in an environment with teacher leaders and leadership of the highest caliber ensures that the work moves forward.

Teachers have four hours of planning time each week when the students attend enrichment classes (garden, art, music, and PE). During that time they create their units of study and projects based on the California State Standards. This may be done with their grade-level team or in their dyad.

Sarah Eun described the process used for her second / third-grade class. "The standards are the skeleton. We start there and see what the students must learn. Then we generate a guiding question and start dialoguing and looking through resources. We ask ourselves how we can make the learning a deeper experience." Within the philosophy of constructivism, teachers do not tell students; they allow students to explore. The focus is not so much about the answer; it's more about using multiple strategies to problem solve and discussing those strategies with peers.

Units of study are interdisciplinary and the projects reflect that philosophy. In the kindergarten-first grade classes, students study habitats. In September they study the school habitat, the routines, procedures, parts of the school, and the people in the school. They read books about it, write about it, and solve problems in math (e.g., How many chairs are there in our school habitat?). Then each of the classes studies a different global habitat. The class studying the desert will build an imaginary animal out of recycled materials. Questions such as: What would it eat in the desert? What kind of mouth does it need to eat that kind of food? What kind of home will it live in? What do the animals do and need to do to live in the desert? Their answers to these questions reflect their mastery of what they've learned about the desert environment.

In the second-third-grade classes, students study simple machines. Given six simple machines, students are not told what they are and how they work. Rather they are put into groups to create their own hypothesis to answer those questions. The culminating project for students is to make their own invention that will make some kind of work easier for themselves and their family and demonstrate their creativity through their ability to write and illustrate their ideas. The project integrates science with English language arts and mathematics.

In fourth grade a project asked students to plan a vacation for their family. Given a $4500 budget, students are given data about how many miles away their California destination was, and the costs of gas, lodging, meals, and admission to attractions. They then have to calculate the cost of their vacation, how long it could be, and how deluxe their accommodations and meals could be. When completed, the students write about why they chose their destination, what it had to offer, and their reason for choosing it. The final step is to create a poster advertising their destination vacation. Social studies, math, ELA, and art are all incorporated into the project.

In math fifth graders apply their skills to research projects. Students research the prices of cat food advertised in different print media. They research a price comparison and determine the best buy. The students are given freedom as to how to present their findings. As fifth-grade teacher Sandra Alamo says, "The skills they're learning connect to the real world, and don't always manifest in a three-dimensional project. The important thing is the process getting there."

Much credit for Larchmont's success may be attributed to the adoption of the Readers and Writers Workshop curricula. The Writer's Workshop is based on Lucy Calkins' work with Teachers' College at Columbia University. Starting with the personal narrative genre, teachers use children's literature and student's own drawings to provide models and prompts for storytelling used to develop authentic writing. Mini lessons, peer and teacher conferencing, and Author's Chair provide multiple opportunities for feedback. Posted written work is everywhere. Students are seen sitting with partners practicing reading their work in preparation for publishing or reading their work to their parents during a celebration of learning.

Over the years teachers have created rubrics for kindergarten through fifth grade and curriculum maps at each grade level. They have relied on each other's expertise to develop curriculum and there is openness about sharing ideas and being observed by other teachers. Teachers also take advantage of Principal Dolores Patton's expertise. She has given them the freedom to research ideas and try them out in the classroom.

Everyone at Larchmont holds high expectations for all students. Larchmont truly believes that their students can learn to the highest level regardless of background, race, ethnicity, socioeconomic status, family support structure, or learning needs. Goals are set around that belief; programs and support are developed around that belief, and instructional strategies are modified when it appears that certain students are not getting what they need.

The fact that a student has an IEP or that parents are not helping at home are never accepted as reasons for students not to succeed. Those are things that are considered helpful information, but the teachers take responsibility to take that information and retool what they're doing to make sure that all students are getting what they need to learn at the highest levels.

There is a seamless feel to the school. Students in any grade can go to any other teacher for help. Teachers don't separate themselves. Everyone's class is everyone's. All teachers have a say in what happens with all students. Teachers can discipline other teachers' students if necessary. Administration encourages teachers to observe peers, take notes, and give each other feedback. Teachers and administrators sub for each other to facilitate observations.

Great teachers and great leadership are essential to Larchmont's success, and all staff is focused on what it will take to get great teachers or great principals in and supporting them. The hiring process is a rigorous one. For teachers, there is a résumé screening, a phone interview, an interview with the principal, a demonstration lesson, an interview with other teachers, and reference checks. For principals, it is a similar process with a great deal of data analysis, reference conversations, and seeing them in the context of their work. Many of the current Larchmont teachers had a long tryout period as substitutes or teacher assistants, so the staff had the opportunity to thoroughly vet them before inviting them to join their community.

According to resource teacher Diane Pullano, "It is the unifying purpose—the mission and philosophy of teaching that really unifies us. That vision determines what the culture is at the school." The teachers agree that it is the same culture that's found in all classrooms, at staff meetings, and before and after school on the yard. The ESLRs (Expected Schoolwide Learning Results) are reinforced in every grade. The ESLRs state that a Larchmont Charter School graduate is a lifelong learner who communicates, seeks to understand, demonstrates respect, takes responsibility, and perseveres.

The younger grades use "cool tools" (metaphors) to help students grasp concepts. For example, to bring home the responsibility ESLR (students take responsibility for one's words), toothpaste is a metaphor for saying something and not being able to take it back. The students do an activity where they try to put the toothpaste back in the tube. The meaning becomes clear: Even if you apologize, you can't take it all back.

Although not part of a formal governance structure (teachers are not required to sit on committees), teachers feel free to voice their opinions, and know their input will be valued. Grounded in data, debates about multilevel classrooms and how the school will grow are common topics. Recently, based on a discussion with the middle school teachers at a kindergarten through eighth grade articulation professional-development session, the dialogue centered on handwriting. The middle school teachers were struggling with students who had illegible penmanship and asked for help. The discussion was rich about the causes and possible action steps that could be taken. Although no decision was reached that day, the process was appreciated. Nora Robinson puts it this way, "We love working here in part because our voices are so valued and we have so much say in what goes on. We can have a two-hour conversation about handwriting, and at the end of the day, if we come to consensus, we can implement that."

FUTURE PLANS

Larchmont Charter School and Larchmont Charter West Hollywood grew over the years to include campuses at Hollygrove, Fairfax, and Selma. In 2011 Larchmont's charter was amended to include a high school and was approved by the LAUSD School Board. Larchmont opened its doors to forty-three ninth graders in the fall of that year. In order to provide an opportunity for all Larchmont students to attend Larchmont Charter High School, all campuses were merged into one organizational structure in July 2013. The new middle and high school campus at La Fayette Park Place opened its doors to grades six through twelve in the fall of 2013, thus providing students with a seamless K–12 curriculum. As Brian Johnson stated, "We believe that we can be a transformative voice in public education in Los Angeles. So the question is, do we stay as a K–12 and be a really good example? Or do we grow multiple clusters?"

The Western Association of Schools and Colleges (WASC) Action Plan identified five areas for improvement: (1) Close the achievement gap between Caucasian and Latino students in math and ELA; (2) Develop a cohesive and responsive professional-development plan; (3) Address issues of space; (4) Develop technology infrastructure, improve hardware and software; and (5) Develop the language of mathematics. These areas will be addressed over the next several years.

Teachers share that they would like to continue to improve their practices; although pleased with what they have achieved, they are never satisfied. As Sarah Eun put it, "Our work is never done. We're aiming for perfection. The students are changing and we have to adapt. Teaching is like a big lab experiment—we're constantly tweaking and changing." As part of this growth, they also expressed the desire to share what they are doing and learn from teachers at other campuses—to have more dialogue in a professional setting.

CONCLUSIONS

Students are provided a challenging, constructivist-based learning environment. All staff is part of a community of professionals dedicated to providing students a world-class education. The culture of the school is one where students feel safe to call their teachers and their principal by their first names.

It doesn't matter that a student is proficient on the CST—Larchmont has higher standards than that. Getting 100 percent is not enough. Was it easy getting that 100 percent? Is there something more that the student could have brought to it? Doing well on a pencil/paper test is not enough: Did the students use higher-level thinking skills? Can they synthesize information? Can they extrapolate from one idea to another? Can they apply what they have learned in a project? Can they diverge in their thinking from one issue to another? The staff is constantly questioning what more they can do to help students rise to the highest levels.

Teachers want the school to maintain the small and cozy feeling they have developed, but as Dolores Patton observes, "We had six hundred applications for sixty-six kindergarten spots. It's hard to look all those families in the face and tell them they can't come here."

KEY ELEMENTS

- Larchmont teachers set academic goals and benchmarks and assess students frequently to determine progress. They then develop curricula to meet students' needs in a constructivist, project-based thematic learning environment.
- The mission and vision of the school serve to unify the staff. A rigorous hiring process ensures that all new staff members are thoroughly vetted and will support the culture of the school.
- The funding priority is hiring personnel in order to keep the student/teacher ratio as low as possible.

CHAPTER 15

Magnolia Science Academy
Reseda, California

INTRODUCTION

Magnolia Science Academy–Reseda (MSA-1) is part of the Magnolia Education & Research Foundation, established in 1997 by a group of community members who saw the need to improve students' achievement in science, technology, engineering, and math (STEM), and inspire students to choose career paths in science and technology. According to Dr. Bahceci, the foundation CEO, "We have to train scientific thinkers because the world is becoming a global business now. Students have to be able to deal with a lot of information flowing around them via the internet and social networks—so we have to respond. We have to give them the opportunity to be scientific critical thinkers with social responsibility."

The founders began to implement their vision by providing free tutoring to middle and high schools in math, science, and computer technology. This program was expanded in 1999 when the foundation implemented a joint program with the Culver City Unified School District to provide tutoring for students in the entire district.

In the fall of 2002 MSA-1 was founded. Originally, the foundation attempted to purchase a property on Magnolia Avenue for the school. Although that purchase fell through, the Magnolia name was retained. Over the last ten years, the foundation has expanded to twelve schools. One school is K–5, two are middle schools, and the rest are grades 6–12. In 2009 the state of California gave the foundation permission to open ten statewide benefit charter schools over the following six years without working within the confines of local school districts.

The foundation is working to replicate the model that has been successful in MSA-1. As Dr. Bahceci puts it, "We do more with less. The central office makes it cost effective and efficient. It's like Starbucks—it's the same wherever you go. There is consistency across the system—the program is the same, but teachers have flexibility to customize. That's what charters are about—teachers have flexibility."

Teacher Alison Brough agrees. "I am free to teach whatever I want as long as it's standards based. Here I can tailor what I do more for my students. This year my sixth-grade class is really low, so I have had to do loads of scaffolding. Because I'm free to go backwards a little, I can pull them up a little."

MSA-1 started in 2002 with two hundred students in grades six through nine, and added a grade level each year. The school is at capacity with a waiting list at every grade, the largest in sixth grade. Currently there are four classes in sixth and seventh grades, three classes in eighth and ninth grades, and two classes each in grades ten through twelve. Class size does not exceed twenty-five. AP classes are even smaller. For example, AP calculus has only fifteen students. Although the school's focus is on math and science, the majority of students come because of siblings, neighbors, and word of mouth.

Principal Mustafa Sahin shares that the majority of entering sixth-grade students come to the school with a second- or third-grade academic level without a strong interest in math or science. The school focuses on "catching them up" and "getting the foundation strong so we can build on that."

The ethnic breakdown of MSA-1's 488 students is 11 percent White, 10 percent Asian/Filipino/Pacific Islander, 78 percent Hispanic, 1 percent African American, and less than 1 percent American Indian. Approximately 90 percent of the students are on the Free and Reduced-Price Lunch Program (Socioeconomically Disadvantaged), 9 percent are ELs, and 14 percent are SWDs.

The school boasts a 100 percent CAHSEE (California High School Exit Exam) passage rate and graduation rate, with 90 percent attending California State universities, universities of California, and private universities. The other 10 percent attend community colleges. MSA-1's API rose from 620 in 2002/2003 to 805 in 2011/2012. The school met all of its AYP indicators.

Data Implications

Year	Enrollment	% AI	% Asian/Filipino/ Pacific Islander	% Black	% Hispanic	% White
			Ethnicity			
2012–13	488	0.4	10.2	1.0	77.5	10.9
2011–12	521	0.8	9.4	0.9	74.5	14.4
2010–11	499	0.8	8.6	1.6	71.1	17.6

Year	% Socioeconomic	% English Learners	% Students w/ Disabilities
2012–13	90.4	9.2	13.6
2011–12	90.0	17.9	12.9
2010–11	84.8	13.6	7.8

Year	API	% AYP—English Lang Arts*	% Mathematics*
2012–13	797	53.0	51.7
2011–12	805	55.8	53.8
2010–11	807	56.2	54.7

* = Percent at/above Proficient

Dr. Bahceci sets the tone for taking data analysis very seriously. "Academia is the number-one priority because otherwise we don't exist. If students are not learning, we are out of business." The entire system starts in the summer looking at the data closely for each student, and moves on to the grade level, classroom level, school level, and CMO level. In the summer of 2011 MSA-1 utilized the Accord Institute to provide data training for each teacher. Teachers received training in ways to "tweak" their curriculum to meet students' individual needs.

Teachers come in three weeks early in the summer for a week of intensive in-service training, and a week when they meet with every student (and their parents) in their homeroom. Based on their ongoing review of data, teachers turn in their annual plans and syllabi to the dean of academics. Lesson plans are turned in biweekly to department chairs and the dean of academics, who meet to review and approve the plans. In addition to school-level analysis of data, every month the principals of all twelve schools meet to analyze and understand all available data, and to share best practices at their sites.

In addition to the CSTs, Measures of Academic Progress (MAP) are administered three times a year. MAP is computer adapted and norm referenced, and is overseen by the Northwest Evaluation Association to provide valuable information to teachers in reading, language usage, and mathematics. Teachers receive the results within twenty-four hours so that students who need remediation and intervention are identified early, and changes to classroom practice may be made immediately.

Students identified as low achieving through MAP test results, low grades, and/or teacher recommendation, participate in free after-school tutoring. These sessions are mandatory and tailored to each student's needs; the tutoring may be once or more a week. Teachers and university volunteers provide tutoring sessions for students individually or in groups not to exceed eight students. Tutoring is part of an improvement plan developed by the teacher, parents, and dean of academics, and may also include additional homework and assignments.

High-performing students are not ignored. Gifted and highly gifted students have the opportunity to compete in prestigious math and science competitions such as the International Mathematics Olympiad, and receive coaching after school and on weekends through the Advanced Math/Science Program. High-achieving students who want more may also participate in tutoring upon request.

SUCCESS FACTORS

All students are required to take four years of mathematics. They take algebra 1 in eighth grade, algebra 2 in ninth grade, then geometry, math analysis, and calculus. There is strong support for math given through after-school tutoring, Saturday school, and intense help during school. If students are struggling in a specific area, they are not allowed to go to electives and must focus on the core. Khan Academy, a computer-based math program, is utilized to make up skills all the way up to calculus.

In science all students are required to take biology, chemistry, and physics. There are two kinds of physics to meet students' needs, but since the goal is to connect students to math and science, these courses are mandatory.

Although the focus is math and science, art, music, and other electives are offered. Spanish and Turkish are offered in middle school, and Spanish is offered in high school.

Technology Integrated Education (TIE©) is a major component of every student's instructional program. Students spend a minimum of five hours a week in front of a computer. Computer classes are integrated into core classes. Once a week, the math, language arts, science, and social science teachers each spend one hour in the computer lab with their students. Core teachers use the computer as a tool to increase the process of learning content standards. After students learn a concept in the class, they go to computer lab for hands-on activities. For example, if students are exploring pressure/volume ratio in class, they can then plot all these data in the computer lab.

Teachers collaborate to integrate technology into all classes, such as: Students will learn how to manipulate an Excel spread sheet; the English teacher then has the students put spelling words in an Excel spreadsheet, and the math teacher has students use math equations in an Excel format. Teachers make connections between technology and everyday life, and feel that it is successful. The grades in the general classes have all increased because of the connection to the computer lab.

For special education, a collaborative model is utilized. Three full-time resource teachers (RSTs) who serve by grade level push into the classroom, but also pull out to a learning center. Students are able to get additional instruction during the elective time unless the teacher and RST collaborate and decide to pull out during cores. The learning center is also open for students before and after school for additional support.

To support language acquisition for ELs and reclassified students, a computer program (Lexia) is being used. A full-time EL teacher pulls out students who are low (especially newcomers) during electives and PE to provide extra support and scaffold learning for core. The EL teacher also provides specialized tutoring after school to support the EL students.

The Get Ready for Life (GRFL) curriculum is provided for middle school students once a week. The purpose is to teach them how to be good citizens—i.e., what the character traits of a good person are. Students are explicitly taught how to be respectful of others. They are taught how to deal with stress and difficult situations. Because many of the students come from families that are gang related, their first reaction to a problem may be the use of violence. GRFL teaches students different ways to approach problems. Music and art are integrated to help make connections for the student. There is a set curriculum that the foundation developed, however the program may be modified as needed. For example, if there is a school shooting, the GRFL teacher will address it immediately.

Part of the character-building process is to connect students to their neighborhood. Every six months there is a neighborhood clean up and at least half of the student body participates. They will pick weeds, paint walls, and do whatever is needed to upgrade their community. Students and their parents participate because they want to, not for extra credit or points. According to Kelly Hourigan, foundation director of special education and discipline, "We're teaching our kids the importance of community. We want them to be an active part of it. It gets them away from negative social pressure such as gangs. It teaches them that they can be successful."

Every classroom has an agenda and the state standards being taught are posted. During the first five minutes of class, students work on a Bellwork assignment. At the end of the lesson, there is a wrap-up to summarize what was done in class that day and set expectations for the next day. There is a set homework policy. Monday and Wednesday are reserved for math and science homework. On Tuesday and Thursday, English and history homework is assigned. Friday is open for all classes. This ensures that students are not overloaded on any one particular day.

Teachers are supported by administration and each other. Teachers have the opportunity to meet with the principal once a week, one-on-one, to discuss successes and needs. Teacher Alison Brough shares, "There's tons of collaboration here—I'm always knocking on my fellow teacher's door to say I'm having a problem with this kid. We really intervene a lot."

Every classroom has a university theme in the homeroom class. The students either choose the university their teacher graduated from or they choose another. They are referred to by that university name all year. For example, the four sixth-grade homerooms are University of California at Los Angeles, University of Southern California, Massachusetts Institute of Technology, and California State University Los Angeles. The students research their universities and fill out an application for that school and submit it to their teacher. They wear their college's gear/colors every Friday. By the time they graduate, they will have participated in seven different universities. The staff found this system very motivating and a major factor in why 100 percent of their students attend college upon graduation.

MSA-1 boasts 150 graduates, most of whom are the first to go to college in their family. A new program was recently instituted whereby MSA-1 alumni are being hired to work at the schools. Depending on where their college is located, students work a few days a week at the school. It keeps them connected to the school, and provides the added benefit of providing role models for the students.

There are numerous enrichment activities available to students such as after-school clubs (theater/film, robotics, scrapbooking, guitar, etc.). Teachers are required to teach one after-school club a week and tutor at least once a week. All students participate in many field trips, including visits to colleges. Contests are instructive but fun. For example, on Pi Day, March 14, there were contests to see which students could memorize the fifty numbers past the decimal in Pi and who could draw a perfect circle freehand closest to Pi.

To make a connection between home life and school, and to introduce themselves, all teachers go on home visits. Most students' homes are visited once a year. For sixth grade, the visits are at the beginning of the year, with the higher-grade students' visits throughout the rest of the year. With the increase in homeless students, accommodations are made at school for these parents' visits. The teachers use this time to talk about the students' progress, interests, and concerns. These visits also give the parents the opportunity to learn more about the school, parent activities, and school events. Parents are encouraged to get involved.

At the same time, parents start to learn about the communication system available to them known as CoolSIS. During the first two months of school, there are trainings (including Saturdays) for parents on how to access the computer system, which serves as their connection to the school. CoolSIS allows parents to have immediate access to their student's courses, grades, discipline entries, communication log, the school calendar, homework, attendance, and the teacher's phone extension and e-mail address. The information is available seven days a week, twenty-four hours a day so it is flexible for the parent's needs.

Also available to parents, and a major part of the culture of the school, is the point system for behavior. Any teacher can go into the system and give positive or negative points or add to the communication log to students or parents. Teacher Alison Brough is pleased with the system and says, "I can see a kid in the hall that's not my kid and say, you just got a negative point, rather than having to track down their teacher. It's easy. You have to be fair and consistent and that helps a lot." One or two points are the most points that teachers can take away or add.

Points are deducted for disrespectful behavior or a uniform infraction, for example. Positive points may be awarded for random acts of kindness, or a good uniform. There are no surprises—behavior expectations are clear. The system is the same in every class on every Magnolia campus. Whenever there is an entry (good or bad), it is automatically e-mailed to parents.

Positive rewards include: +5—Contact parents; +10—Certificate and treat; +15—One free slice of pizza; +20—One free dress pass; +25—Ice cream party; +30—Entered in a raffle for lunch with a teacher; +35—Entered in a raffle for a gift card; +40—Free dress every Friday for one month; +45—Recognized at assembly and a treat; and +50—special VIP treat for you and a guest. Negative consequences include: −5—Contact parent; −10—Behavior plan and loss of privileges (no assembly, no free dress, no after-school clubs); −15—Red slip and assigned table at lunch with a teacher; −20—Lunch inside (no outside time); −25—Saturday school; −30—One day in school suspension and counseling; −35—Parent attends school the entire day with student; −40—One day at-home suspension: −45—Two day at-home suspension; and −50—Discipline committee to discuss possible expulsion. At the end of the year, the student with the highest number of points receives an iPad.

FUTURE PLANS

The Magnolia Foundation's application to the California Commission on Teacher Credentialing was approved to be a credentialing agency for its own teachers. This has not been implemented yet, but the first step of formulating an advisory board has been accomplished.

Although the foundation has permission to grow ten more schools in six years, the plan is to move slowly and deliberately. Past experience has shown that when resources are poured into a new school, the rest of the schools may suffer. The Magnolia Schools' average API scores over the years demonstrate this. From 2002 to 2005, the scores rose. When a second school was added in 2006, the scores flattened. In 2007 they rose for both schools, and dipped in 2008 when another school was added. This pattern has continued with every new addition, so "caution" is the watchword.

CONCLUSIONS

The MSA model is working regardless of the students' income level. The model allows all students to achieve regardless of whether they are English learners or students with disabilities. It is an individualized approach to education. The goal is to meet all students' needs by identifying who they are, what they need, and then paying individual attention to each student's needs. Dr. Bahceci sums it up: "When I talk to principals, I become emotional because I worry about those kids. They are from low-income, maybe single-parent homes. They don't have enough parent support. This is a pipeline to prison! We have to break this pipeline! We have to send them to high levels—we don't have the luxury to sit down here and complain. It's about contributing back to the community."

The faculty at the school brings alumni and their families back for events to keep them connected to the community. As Kelly Hourigan says, "We all just pitch in. It's a family—like a second home—a family-oriented place. Most of the kids come to us with Ds and Fs. We're really getting them to believe in themselves, and that they're able to achieve."

Several MSA-1 students echoed these sentiments. "It's a big family. We can go to any teacher and tell them anything. The help is there. It's just for you to take it." Another student put it this way, "There are so many programs available. There's math club, robotics club, student government. There's somewhere you can fit in. There's a lot of freedom to choose. There's no reason to be left out."

KEY ELEMENTS

- Technology Integrated Education (TIE©) has been a successful strategy that integrates computer education/use with all core curricular areas.
- CoolSIS and the behavior point system provide parents information about their student's progress at anytime day or night. Teachers make home visits to ensure that parents are active partners in their children's education.
- A strong college-going culture exists and contributes to 100 percent of the graduates attending college.

CHAPTER 16

Our Community School
Chatsworth, California

INTRODUCTION

Our Community Charter School (OCS) was founded in 2005 when the Valley Community Charter School's (VCCS) charter was not renewed by LAUSD. Poor test scores for the demographics and a lack of a focus on standards were cited as the reasons. When a campaign to keep the school open failed, Christine Ferris and a few other teachers and parents decided to write their own charter application. Building on the good things that were happening at VCCS, Ms. Ferris took the lead in rewriting the charter and added new curriculum, assessments, and a new governance structure.

The new charter was approved at the end of May, and the next fall reopened with all new board members and a new administrative team in the same location. VCCS had been housed at a church with excellent facilities (classrooms, bathrooms with handicapped stalls, soccer field), and turned over the assets (furniture, books, blocks, etc.) to the new school.

The new school opened with 170 students in grades kindergarten to six. The board's vision of having two teachers per grade level to facilitate collaboration, and give students the opportunity of working in different social groups, was not realized until five years later when OCS moved to its current location.

In the process of searching for a new location, a deserted LAUSD campus only three miles from the church location was identified. Ms. Ferris identified this at the "perfect storm" of factors coming together to win the location for OCS: OCS had just won the Charter School of the Year honor from the California Charter School Association; LAUSD had just lost a Proposition 39 lawsuit; and an LAUSD board member had campaigned on reopening schools in the valley.

Ms. Ferris and the parents campaigned in the neighborhood, the Neighborhood Council, the Chamber of Commerce, and California State University Northridge (CSUN) and received letters of support from them saying that they wanted to reopen the school. OCS moved into the Devonshire site the same year they had to renew their charter (2009/2010) and after LAUSD renovated the campus (it had been closed for thirty years).

Because parents asked for it, and a Harvard study showed that kindergarten through grade-eight schools are good for the middle-school-aged student socially and academically, seventh and eighth grade were added to the charter. In addition, a preference for low-income families (as measured by free and reduced-price lunch eligible) was inserted in the charter's lottery process because so many more middle class families were applying. The school markets itself to low-income families through mailers, visits to local Head Start schools, the website, and word of mouth.

According to Ms. Ferris, "I want them to know this is an option for them. They're looking at a school that's not really serving their kids. Some of the other families that choose us may like our philosophy, but their child would still have learned to read at other neighborhood schools. We're about the mixed group. I feel it's beneficial for kids to have that range—the kids with more middle class backgrounds learn some things about how lucky they are in the world from having friends who are in much more difficult situations. The ethnic diversity is fantastic—that's one of the beautiful things about our school."

OCS finished its third year at the new site in June of 2013. Every year there are two hundred applicants for the forty-four kindergarten slots, and the school maintains a wait list of over three hundred for all grades. Siblings do receive preference in order to keep families together.

The ethnic breakdown of OCS's 397 students is 58 percent White, 28 percent Hispanic, 5 percent Black, 8 percent Asian/Filipino/Pacific Islander, and less than 1 percent American Indian. Approximately 40 percent of the students are on the Free and Reduced-Price Lunch Program (Socioeconomically Disadvantaged), 6 percent are ELs, and 9 percent are SWDs.

Data Implications

			Ethnicity			
Year	Enrollment	% AI	% Asian/Filipino/ Pacific Islander	% Black	% Hispanic	% White
2012–13	392	0.5	7.7	5.4	28.1	58.2
2011–12	334	0.6	6.9	5.1	23.7	62.6
2010–11	322	1.2	9.0	9.3	36.0	42.9

Year	% Socioeconomic	% English Learners	% Students w/ Disabilities
2012–13	40.1	5.6	8.9
2011–12	41.6	4.8	11.3
2010–11	41.9	13.2	8.5

Year	API	% AYP—English Lang Arts*	% Mathematics*
2012–13	864	72.3	64.6
2011–12	872	71.8	70.4
2010–11	852	62.5	73.3

* = Percent at/above Proficient

OCS's API rose from 716 in 2005/2006 to 864 in 2012/2013. However, in 2010, the school only met sixteen of seventeen AYP goals and was put at risk for entering No Child Left Behind Program Improvement (PI) status. The goal of 56.8 percent proficient and advanced on the CST was not met by the Hispanic population (47.6 percent). In 2011 OCS met its AYP goals for their Hispanic and school-wide subgroups through the Safe Harbor provision of demonstrating progress of moving students to proficient and advanced. Unfortunately, the Socioeconomically Disadvantaged subgroup failed to meet AYP by scoring 55.4 percent (goal 67.6 percent). Therefore, OCS entered PI year-one status in 2011/2012.

The school looked closely at the data that put them into PI status. Having done better in mathematics, they attributed that success to their math program of Singapore Math in kindergarten through fifth grade, and Connected Math in grades six and seven. The school used a rigorous selection process that lasted two years before Singapore Math was adopted for implementation.

With a new language arts adoption coming up, the school spent a year researching what would help them close the gap. Ms. Ferris researched different programs and brought the information to the teachers. They talked, brainstormed, and charted the strengths and weaknesses of the program and how well they matched the school's mission and the weaknesses they wanted to improve.

At the conclusion of this process, the school adopted Pearson's Good Habits Great Readers and Words Their Way, which assist teachers in leveling reading groups and teaching comprehension strategies. The series assesses comprehension levels in fiction and nonfiction and students' ability to extract information and summarize it to understand main ideas. Ms. Ferris shares, "The way teachers are writing and talking about reading comprehension, I feel like we're at a whole different level." ELA results for the 2012/2013 CSTs revealed that 72 percent of the students scored at or above proficiency—about a nine-point gain over the previous year.

Every year when the test scores come in, Ms. Ferris utilizes Data Director to upload and analyze scores for the whole school, subgroups, and grade-level teams. She also reviews individual teachers' scores to identify trends. For example, one year she discovered that the language conventions score was lower than the other ELA scores for third grade. She worked with the third-grade team to pull CST release questions on language conventions, and supported their growth in that particular area.

A four-week summer school session is offered for struggling students to work on skill development. It is run for approximately forty students with three teachers (one class each for second/third, fourth/fifth, and sixth/seventh). In addition, tutoring is offered for students who have scored below and far below basic on the CSTs. Small groups of six to ten students receive assistance before and after school two days a week.

There are benchmark assessments three times a year that are tied to the teacher-evaluation process. Teachers are required to carefully evaluate their students' progress as measured by these assessments and reflect on the choices they need to make to do things differently to improve their students' learning. They must turn these written reflections into the principal.

Ms. Ferris shares that she has been pleased with the level of specificity contained in these reflections. "They've gotten so much better. They used to be vague when we first started. Now they can identify very specifically what they're going to do the next couple of weeks that they're going to target as a result of the assessment. They're giving me information on how they're able to reflect and implement choices on what they've learned."

In addition to the principal's evaluation, parents and students have the opportunity to evaluate their teachers by survey. Teachers participate in professional development eight days before the first day of school. These eight days comprise planning, setting up the classrooms, meeting with grade-level partners, and trainings. The trainings are based on the data to determine the focus for the year. For example, professional development on the new English language arts curriculum and assessment was essential based on the school's entrance into PI status. Likewise, the school had trainers from UCLA come to share effective strategies for ELs, based on the deficits identified by assessment data (CST and benchmark).

In addition to the eight days before school, there are five more professional development days throughout the year. Teachers also have the opportunity to attend off-campus professional development. Each teacher is given up to three released days that do not count against their personal days. A component of the professional-development program is collaboration with other charter schools (Synergy, and New Heights, for example) to share best practices.

SUCCESS FACTORS

The curriculum at OCS is divided into three parts: math, language arts, and integrated humanities. Using a backwards planning process (Understanding by Design), teachers examine the standards for social studies, science, and language arts to find connections and create rich project-based units. Teachers ask themselves what is really worth spending time thinking about, discussing, and researching, and how the skills students need to learn fit into that larger unit.

In kindergarten and first grade, an integrated humanities lesson is based around animals. They begin by studying pets and answer such questions as: What pets do you have? What pets could we have in our classroom? What does a pet need to survive? Then they look at working animals such as Seeing Eye dogs and dairy cows. They move on to research wild animals and animals in zoos. As a culmination of this study, the students do their own wild-animal study, write a mini research paper, and create a mask of their animal. They then open their own natural history museum for a day and invite all of the parents to attend. They have to read their report aloud to the parents and answer questions about their animals.

An example of a fifth-grade unit is the study of American history through the frame of technology's effect on historical events. Students examine how navigation tools made it possible for exploration, how the American Revolution was impacted by the printing press, and how the Internet today is impacting the world. In sixth grade, students work on one unit all year, examining ancient history through the lens of culture. The culminating activity asks them to write about what should go in a time capsule that would help explain our culture today. Teachers create projects that make content come alive for students and to help them understand cause-and-effect relationships and think critically about what they are learning.

All teachers are trained in Responsive Classrooms (RC). RC is a classroom-management system that is based on ethical development and teaching children to be good citizens in the community. It teaches them to be empathetic to others' needs as well as their own, and to work collaboratively to fulfill those needs. The first six weeks of school are spent creating community in the classroom, and the focus is social not academic. Students create their own rules for the classroom and agree on the consequences for not following them. Lessons presented daily help students to know each other well and to be comfortable taking academic risks.

Listening and speaking are practiced every day in ways that help students value and respect each other. Founding teachers Catherine Campbell and John Foley believe that RC is fundamental to OCS's success and something that sets the school apart from other schools. As Mr. Foley puts it, "We have a culture here where we don't have to be on page x on date x in our textbooks—no pacing plan. So if there's a problem with a kid in the class, or a group of children, we can stop and deal with it, even if it takes a day or two days. We can stop and deal with the social issues that are going on in the classroom because the social issues are as important as the academic." Ms. Campbell continues, ". . . if not more. Because if there's a fight out on the yard, you cannot be teaching adding fractions when they come back. The whole class is upset and angry. They're involved in whatever happened on the field and they want to talk about it and deal with the situation. They're not able to concentrate on academics."

Mr. Foley adds, "A sense of 'I matter' is instilled from the first day they walk into kindergarten until when they leave in eighth grade. We do it in lots of different ways and they are empowered in many ways. But they really know that they're safe and their feelings matter. That translates in classroom management being much easier. It translates into kids that feel safe and produce better in school—they're willing to take risks and so can do more in the classroom."

Every morning, during the first twenty minutes of school, every class holds a "Morning Meeting." These twenty minutes provide students the opportunity to connect and transition into a productive school day. Everyone gets greeted individually by name and then share in some kind of fun activity and a message that launches them into their academics.

Students are taught "I" messages and practice them in the Peaceful Learning Communities (PLC). This may occur every day in the early grades to a few times a week in the upper grades. These are meetings where students are given the opportunity to share a variety of concerns. The meetings start out with appreciating. Students make statements such as, "I like the way you sit next to me at lunch and how we play at recess." Then the problem is stated, "Today when we were playing soccer and I missed the ball and fell down you laughed at me and it really hurt my feelings." The third part is stating what is desired, "I'd really like for you to not tease me anymore."

Teachers work to provide a safe environment so that every child has a voice at OCS. Students feel comfortable speaking in class (in academics), and during PLCs. Biweekly assemblies provide a natural platform for students to share with the school community and community at large. Classrooms take turns hosting and are completely in charge from emceeing to maintaining discipline. Classes share skits, songs, dances, announcements, and share the work they're doing in their classes. Parents are encouraged to attend. Within a one- or two-year span, every student will get up on stage and speak in front of the school.

OCS is committed to providing a program that balances academics with creativity. All classes have weekly music lessons. Students in kindergarten through fourth grade learn singing and xylophones. Fifth- and sixth-grade students learn to play drums and guitar, and then perform at the House of Blues (part of the House of Blues Foundation). Seventh- and eighth-grade students are offered guitar skills and music history as electives. A parent group of volunteers organized themselves and wrote standards-based lesson plans in visual arts and teach the kindergarten through sixth-grade students once a month. Seventh and eighth graders also have visual arts offered as an elective.

A rigorous hiring process ensures that teachers are a good fit for the OCS philosophy. Ms. Ferris sends out questions to those teachers whose résumés appear promising. She then provides the candidate with a tour of the school and shares OCS's vision and mission with them. Those that make the cut teach a demonstration lesson with an OCS class in front of a panel that includes administration, teachers (the other teacher on the grade level is mandatory), and parents or board members. The panel interviews the candidate after the lesson, asking questions such as "What do you think went well? What would you do differently? What is your philosophy about teaching?" The entire panel must agree to hire, or they keep looking. Six of the original eight teachers are still part of the staff.

All classes are required to do a minimum of three field trips a year, which must be tied to the curriculum. When doing their animal study, kindergarten visits a neighborhood pet store, the zoo, the Long Beach Aquarium, and a farm. The fifth grade goes to Riley's Farm in Riverside for a colonial reenactment. Second grade's "Farm to Family" unit is enriched by trips to the grocery store, a farmers' market, and a working farm. Ms. Ferris states, "There is a strong belief that students learn out in the world, not just in a classroom from pictures in a book."

The sixth grade presents plays about ancient civilizations that they have written and directed themselves. The performance serves as a fund-raiser to support the sixth-grade trip to the Grand Canyon Observatory in Arizona to participate in an archeological dig—looking for pottery shards ten thousand years old.

Parents are an integral component of OCS's success. Not only do they teach music and visual arts to the students, but they also run a gardening program that teaches the students about organic gardening and seed harvesting. As Ms. Ferris elaborates, "We wouldn't be in this location without our parents' commitment and campaign that they did. We wouldn't have opened to start with; we wouldn't have the amount of fund-raising that we do and we wouldn't have the amount of richness in our curriculum. It's really because they feel that they are part of this place. That's part of our name—why it's called Our Community—because it's all of ours and we're making it work together."

Also integral to OCS are the partnerships established with community organizations. The Kinesiology and Visual/Performing Arts Departments of CSUN work with OCS students in physical education and the arts. In addition, the school partners with the Mitchell Family Center for family counseling, neighborhood councils, Kiwanis, two Chambers of Commerce in the San Fernando Valley, Whole Foods, and MSM Technology. The school lives up to its "Our Community" name.

FUTURE PLANS

The school is maxed out on space, and cannot add classes. Concerned with budget cuts, the school is doing everything possible to avoid increasing class sizes (twenty-two in kindergarten and twenty-five in the other grades). A development director was hired to maximize fundraising. As Ms. Ferris comments, "Parents do a lot, but we are hoping to bump it up so we can stay where we want to be—not to add, but not to have to cut back on things." At present, there is no plan to grow, either by adding students at OCS or by adding new sites.

CONCLUSIONS

OCS has created an educational environment that integrates rigorous academics and creative project-based units with meticulous attention to students' social and emotional growth. Responsive Classrooms and Peaceful Learning Communities help students become empathetic problem solvers. Students feel valued and truly part of the community. Students and adults alike address each other by first name, and uniforms are not required. It is most telling that administrators and teachers have their own children enrolled at OCS. Teacher John Foley sums it up: "It's been an amazing journey being part of the creation of something that's trying to make a difference in education. We are trying to set a model on how to work with children that's different—respectful. And we've done that."

KEY ELEMENTS

- The social and emotional development of students is treated as important as academic growth. The tenets of the Responsive Classrooms and Peaceful Learning Communities programs have formed a strong foundation for students' success.
- Benchmark assessments given three times a year are tied to teacher evaluation. Teachers must reflect on the data and turn in specific plans to improve student outcomes.
- The community as a whole, which includes parents, businesses, organizations, and the local university, all contribute to the success of the school.

CHAPTER 17

Vaughn Next Century Learning Center
Pacoima, California

INTRODUCTION

In 1990 when Dr. Yvonne Chan arrived at Vaughn Elementary School, a LAUSD school in Pacoima, she was faced with what seemed to be insurmountable odds. The students were performing in the single digits on standardized tests. The school was on a Concept 6 multitrack calendar, which meant that students were only receiving 163 days of instruction instead of 180. In spite of the year-round schedule, 270 students had to be bused to other schools.

The school's student demographics were 100 percent socioeconomically disadvantaged, and 80 percent ELs. Her staff had an annual 30–40 percent turnover rate, and 60 percent were emergency credentialed teachers. As Dr. Chan tells it, "The rest were old and ready to retire." Seven or eight staff members were out on workers' compensation every day. As she puts it, "I was hired because I was a first-generation immigrant, fluent in Spanish, of a neutral race and had adequate experience. I wasn't hired because I had been a bilingual teacher, a central office administrator, an administrator over special education, and had a doctorate from UCLA and eight credentials from CSUN."

The school's racial demographic had been primarily African American, but over time the racial and ethnic balance changed radically. The neighborhood was filled with struggling, undocumented immigrant families living in dilapidated housing. The black/brown issues were putting a stranglehold on any possible improvement at Vaughn. The previous principal (Hispanic) had gone out on disability because of death threats.

The school had been at the bottom of lowest-performing schools for twenty years when Dr. Chan took over. She vowed to bring the community back together by having them work together on some quick fixes to make the campus safe. She got the Hispanic parents who were day laborers to build fences and plant grass, and the African American parents joined in and helped. Over time, the projects helped to unite the two groups and created momentum and energy by showing them what they could accomplish together. She spent two and a half years on these projects—window dressing as she called them—and started to create a common mission.

Vaughn's teachers were frustrated with LAUSD's bilingual education mandates. The bilingual teachers were ending up with forty-five ELs in a class while the English-only teachers had only twenty students. This provided the impetus for a new plan. Dr. Chan led the teachers in the development of a school-based management plan that addressed a basic issue: The school wanted control over their EL funding and positions. This would ensure that positions would be in place to support ELs, there would be no split grades, and a systematic teaming plan could be put in place. LAUSD and United Teachers of Los Angeles both rejected their proposal. Dr. Chan says that the push back was disappointing and insulting but primarily based in the politics of the time.

Dr. Chan attended a conference entitled "Autonomy with Accountability" and shared the information with her staff. She told them that they must have "high collective expectations that we can do the impossible." Eighty-six percent of the staff was in favor of applying for charter school status. They wrote a twenty- to thirty-page charter proposal that outlined how to do transitional English, how to implement teaming, how to collapse the split grade-level classes, and how to deploy finances.

In addition to a $175,000 loan from the Los Angeles County Office of Education, Dr. Chan mortgaged her house to get liability insurance, and cashed a Certificate of Deposit to pay the union dues. The Vaughn Next Century Learning Center (VNCLC) opened in July 1993 with thirty-six teachers, one principal, one assistant principal, and two coordinators (there are now 130 certificated employees). VNCLC became the first conversion charter school in the nation with admission preference given to neighborhood children.

In 1996 VNCLC (Mainland) purchased a lot adjacent to the school and added fourteen new classrooms, which allowed the school to go off of the year-round calendar. In 2000 Panda Pavilion was built on another adjacent lot purchased to provide a new community library, clinic, museum, multimedia lab, science center, professional-development center, and demonstration classrooms.

In 2003 land was purchased to build PandaLand for a 650-seat primary center to house prekindergarten, kindergarten, and first grade. In 2006 land across the street was purchased to build Panda Academy for a five hundred-student high school focusing on international studies and world languages. From being helpless and hopeless in 1993, the school has grown to be the heart of the community and has won numerous awards including the California Distinguished Schools Award in 1996 and the National Blue Ribbon Schools Award in 1997.

Dr. Chan retired, but has remained on as VNCLC's founding principal and visionary officer. She is paid a dollar per year, and says that she is there to keep the mission and vision on course, which included taking the whole staff to China on spring break 2012. She prepared the school for the transition by exercising a distributive leadership model.

Data Implications

			Ethnicity			
Year	Enrollment	% AI	% Asian/Filipino/ Pacific Islander	% Black	% Hispanic	% White
2012–13	2429	0	0.3	0.7	98.6	0.3
2011–12	2259	0	0.4	0.8	98.5	0.4
2010–11	2209	0	0.3	1.0	98.3	0.3

Year	% Socioeconomic	% English Learners	% Students w/ Disabilities
2012–13	99.0	23.5	8.6
2011–12	99.7	26.4	10.4
2010–11	96.3	31.7	9.7

Year	API	% AYP—English Lang Arts*	% Mathematics*
2012–13	832	58.0	71.1
2011–12	821	58.2	62.5
2010–11	816	55.8	62.9

* = Percent at/above Proficient

Over the five-year period before retirement, she carefully moved her responsibilities to the new principal, Anita Zepeda.

The current school enrollment for K–12 is 2,429 with an additional enrollment of 330 pre-K students. Of those K–12 students, 99 percent are Hispanic; only seventeen students (1 percent) are "other." Students in the Free and Reduced-Price Lunch Program (Socioeconomically Disadvantaged) comprise 99 percent; 24 percent are ELs and 9 percent are SWDs.

From the inception of API in 1999, VNCLC's ratings have made amazing gains. From a score of 443 in 1999, their API is now 832. In 2005 VNCLC failed to meet their AMOs, and in 2011 became a Program Improvement 5 school. However, in 2011, they met their AMOs through Safe Harbor by demonstrating progress in moving students from scoring at the below-proficient level to the proficient level. The AMOs not met consistently involved the EL subgroup and most recently included the school-wide, and the Hispanic, Socioeconomically Disadvantaged in the area of mathematics. Since these groups comprise at least 99 percent of their population, VNCLC is continuing to focus on their data and providing relevant professional development for all teachers.

SUCCESS FACTORS

Shared governance is key to VNCLC's success. All teachers are required to serve on a committee that not only gives input, but has final decision-making power. Teachers say they have buy-in because they have that power. There are three committees: Curriculum and Instruction (C & I), Business, and Partnership. C & I drives the other committees. The committees make decisions about instructional needs and practices, finances, parent and community outreach, and how resources are brought in. Everything that the committees do is based on the mission and vision of the school, which are constantly revisited.

Not part of the governance structure is the Bureau of Student Affairs, which is in charge of student activities and cultural events such as science fairs, spelling bees, performances, and parades. This committee serves as an entry-level committee for new teachers before they sit on a governance committee. There is representation from all grade levels on all of the committees, and they have the responsibility to communicate back to their constituents.

Decisions about professional development (PD) come from the C & I committee and administrative staff working together collaboratively, and are always based on data. Each administrator is responsible for a group of teachers and sits in on grade-level meetings (clan meetings) to articulate needs and help develop plans. During these meetings they discuss issues, problem solve, and set goals. Administrators then meet to share concerns; this in turn informs decisions about PD.

There is trust between teachers and administrators. As Executive Director Anita Zepeda tells it, "We trust each other. We are all professionals seeking the same goals. With transparency and sharing of facts, I trust that our staff is capable of generating informed, healthy, and appropriate decision-making. Sometimes I may not agree 100 percent with decisions made, but often I'm surprised by the great perspectives brought to the table." She continues, "Teachers are able to teach their grade level or content area and in addition wear another hat and make decisions or draft policies much like an administrator. They're able to see the needs of the whole school, not just that of their own class. It's a great development of the talent within a charter that happens when you allow them to be the professionals driving the instruction of the whole school. It's beautiful!"

Teachers also feel that trust. They have no qualms talking to their administrators and have confidence that they will be supported. They are willing to admit that they need help and can talk about any issue at any hour of the day. Administrators are available by phone and e-mail well after hours.

The clans (grade levels) meet every week to collaborate on developing lessons, but there are also teams (subgroups of the grade level). This is where the teachers get to know their students in depth. Students do not belong to just one teacher; all the team members share responsibility for all students' growth. For differentiation, teachers employ flexible groupings so that one teacher teaches students who need to be challenged while another teammate teaches students who need extra support and might co-teach with the resource teacher. Lessons are accommodated to meet students' needs. There is additional intervention during the day during teaming, and tutoring after school.

Excellent financial management has allowed VNCLC to keep class sizes small, and to add additional days to the school year; the school operates on a 195-day schedule instead of 180 days. Dr. Chan shared that the school has an annual budget of $24 million and has more than $84 million in assets. The school is even able to sell its own bonds.

Everyone agrees that success is impossible without the best teaching staff available. The teachers shared this insight. "If your passion isn't here then you don't belong here. People don't come here for the money—they're here because they love to teach children. We have teachers who have the passion. And the ones who didn't, they're not here anymore. And that's why when you hear all the years that people have been here, it's because we have it. Dr. Chan says that this is not the place for the faint of heart because it's too hard to work here—it's not only for the passion, but it's that we built this place together."

To ensure that the right teachers are in place, there is a rigorous hiring procedure. The Personnel Committee, a subcommittee under the C & I Committee, is responsible for the process. The committee screens applications, and conducts a structured interview. Successful candidates must then present demonstration lessons while selected committee members observe and evaluate performance. The Personnel Committee holds the decision-making power. It is interesting to note that students are a part of the hiring process for middle and high school teacher candidates.

Teachers who are not meeting VNCLC's high standards are given the opportunity to improve. Executive Director Anita Zepeda asks the question, "Would I/you have my own children or loved ones in this teacher's class?" At the first level, administrators and an assigned peer provide support through individual assistance, by sending teachers to workshops and by providing opportunities to observe other teachers. At the second level, the administrators and peer provide more intensive support. The third level is dismissal.

Unique to VNCLC is their internal accountability system that provides performance pay incentives to teachers. The Peer Assistance and Review (PAR) evaluation process is complex and differentiated for apprentice teachers (teachers in their first two years of teaching) and regular K–12 teachers.

During the first semester, the PAR process is divided into three components. The first is a pre-visit conference where the administrator and peer evaluator meet with the teacher being evaluated. During this conference the following items are discussed:

- Anything that would assist in establishing a relationship of trust and understanding
- Concerns, apprehensions, needs
- Teacher's description of the program
- Teacher's self-evaluation and description of strengths and weaknesses
- Teacher's description of overall focus and objectives for the year
- Evaluators' description of exemplars and evidence expectations
- Opportunities for teaming

The second component comprises informal observations and assistance. Using checklists and/or *Observation Standards for the Teaching Profession* (Marzano, Frontier & Davidson, 2011), classroom visits are made to check for evidence of expected instructional practices. After the observation(s), the evaluators (administrator and peer) and teacher meet to discuss the evidence collected, provide feedback, and determine assistance as needed. The peer evaluator, administrator, and teacher all sign the checklist/observation instrument, and a signed copy is given to the teacher.

The third component of the PAR evaluation process is observation/evaluation. The administrator and peer evaluator continue to visit and check for evidence of practices directly related to the PAR matrix, which is based on Charlotte Danielson's (2007) *Enhancing Professional Practice: A Framework for Teaching*. The matrices are differentiated for the apprentice teachers and the regular K–12 teachers. In addition to the formal PAR matrix, which is filled out by the evaluators, the teacher also completes a self-evaluation using the rubric. The PAR matrix for the apprentice teacher examines the following domains:

Domain I—Planning and Preparation: instructional materials and resources; lesson and unit structure and planning; and Instructional groups.

Domain II—The Classroom Environment: management of instructional groups; management of transitions and materials/supplies; supervision/collaboration with support staff/paraprofessionals; behavioral expectations; monitoring of student behavior; and response to student misbehavior.

Domain III—Representation of content; activities and assignments; and delivery and pacing.

Domain IV—Professional Responsibilities: self-reflection; accuracy; attends scheduled meetings; punctuality and adheres to work hours; uses illness/release days with discretion; prepares lesson plans for substitute teacher; adheres to dress code per handbook; and professional conduct.

In addition to the above components, the regular K–12 teacher with more than two years of teaching experience is expected to demonstrate deeper knowledge and skill. Their matrix includes:

Domain I—Preparation and Planning: knowledge of content and prerequisite skills; knowledge of varied approaches to learning; awareness of students' skills and knowledge; value, clarity, and suitability of objectives; criteria and standards for assessment; and assessment and evaluation.

Domain II—The Classroom Environment: teacher-student interaction and student-student interaction; service to the student (health, socioemotional); expectations for learning and achievement; and safety, arrangement of furniture, and use of physical resources.

Domain III—Instruction: directions and procedures; providing feedback to students; lesson adjustments; and modifications and flexibility.

Domain IV—Professional Responsibilities: student completion of assignments; student progress in learning; noninstructional records (attendance, registers, Student Success Team (SST) updates, referrals); information about individual students; engagement of families in the instructional program; service to the school; and service to the profession.

Each of the above components of the PAR matrix is evaluated using a four-point scale: innovating (4), integrating (3), basic (2), and unsatisfactory (1). For example, the rubric scale for Domain I, knowledge of varied approaches to learning, is as follows:

Innovating (4)—Teacher consistently uses appropriate knowledge of students' varied approaches to learning in instructional planning, including those with specialized needs; teacher consistently differentiates instruction using a variety of instructional tools.

Integrating (3)—Teacher uses different approaches/strategies for learning to meet students' diverse needs; consistent in use of some instructional tools, checks for understanding, connects to prior knowledge, use of charts, Thinking Maps, graphic organizers, and other scaffolds, as well as technology.

Basic (2)—Teacher displays general understanding of the different approaches to learning that students exhibit and uses some approaches or strategies with mixed results.

Unsatisfactory (1)—Teacher is unfamiliar with the different approaches to learning that students exhibit, such as learning styles, modalities, and multiple "intelligences."

At the end of each semester, teachers' evaluation scores, based on the PAR matrix are provided by the administrator, peer, and self. The three scores are averaged and teachers receive their results in December with related bonuses paid in January. The process is repeated in the second semester with the results provided in June and bonuses paid in July.

Teachers must receive an average score of three or better to receive the extra pay. Year one apprentice teachers may receive up to $2800 for their scores on the matrix; year two teachers may receive up to $4000; and regular K–12 teachers may receive up to $6550. In addition, regular teachers may receive an additional $3000 for their students meeting benchmarks each semester. Both apprentice and regular K–12 teachers receive additional bonuses for student attendance ($500 for a 97 percent attendance rate or $1000 for a 98 percent attendance rate). API goals are set, and all teachers may qualify for an additional $2000 if those goals are met. All teachers also qualify for an additional $1000 for a 90 percent graduation rate.

FUTURE PLANS

Dr. Chan is proud that "we have saturated this high-poverty area to create an education corridor. Herrick Avenue is Vaughn World!" However, in the next breath she says, "You never say you've arrived at the top of the mountain. There's always another mountain." In addition to building another elementary site, she sees the growth of media production. In addition, more technology and STEM research needs to be explored.

At each step of the way as grade levels were added to the original K–6 school, VNCLC was responding to the community's pleas to ensure that their children could continue to attend this safe and high-performing school as they matriculated to the next level. Now that students are graduating from the high school, they are asking if the Vaughn New Century Learning Community College will become a reality. Dr. Chan agrees that that would be the next logical step.

CONCLUSIONS

The VNCLC is a full-service community-based K–12 charter school that has become the heart of the community and transformed the Pacoima area where it is situated. The growth of the school has resulted in a safe and clean neighborhood with reduced graffiti, gang gathering, and gang affiliation among the residents. There is a school-based health clinic staffed by the Los Angeles County Department of Health. A family center provides varied services to the parents, including educational classes, counseling services, temporary assistance and referrals to meet basic needs, computer lab services, and more.

Property has been acquired to build a new family center so that more parents can be served. Vaughn provides jobs to residents including many of VNCLC's former students and their families. For example, several of the school's secretaries are parents of current and former Vaughn students; several of the janitors are parents of current and former students. There are a number of Vaughn alumni now teaching at the school. This all has contributed to a healthier, more resilient, and economically viable community.

The vision that Dr. Chan fostered continues today with passionate teachers who do whatever it takes to ensure student success. The governance structure and PAR process hold teachers to the highest standards and reward them financially when they reach them.

The motto of "Be safe, be respectful and be responsible" is taught and reiterated in every way. The students are safe, respectful, and responsible, and increasing their academic achievement annually. Vaughn Next

Century Learning Center has become a model for school reform locally, nationally, and globally.

KEY ELEMENTS

- VNCLC is a full-service facility that serves students and families in all areas—education, health, and welfare.
- The inclusive governance structure has created a culture of commitment by all staff members.
- The PAR evaluation process not only evaluates teachers, but also supports them in improving their practice and incentivizes them financially to make that improvement.

Conclusion

This anthology is about seventeen Los Angeles charter schools that are making a tremendous difference in the lives of 10,034 students who attend these highly successful schools. They are representative of the many fine public schools in the nation, and can serve as a model for those who are struggling to meet the needs of urban children. The teachers, staff, and administrators of these schools have faced myriad obstacles and challenges as they endeavored to develop and operate charter schools, yet they persevered with a singular purpose in mind: to provide a high-quality educational experience for all students regardless of their background or economic circumstance.

These schools are relentless in their determination to provide all students with a rigorous college-preparatory curriculum. There is a "can-do" culture that permeates these schools, and nothing will get in their way to prevent them from achieving their goals. The teachers, staff, and administrators who work in them are truly educational pioneers.

There are many lessons that can be learned from each of these schools' successes. Most importantly there is a commonality among them. There are essential elements in place in each that make them outstanding schools.

- The schools are built on a foundation of a purposeful vision that is shared by all and supported by the entire school community. The school leader demonstrates a passion for the mission and vision of the school, and influences others to share that vision. The leader also serves as a buffer for outside elements that would detract from

the ability of the teachers and staff to achieve the school's vision, and he or she is able to leverage resources to attain the mission.
- Teachers and staff who work in these schools are carefully selected through a rigorous hiring process. The person or committee who hires new employees looks for people who will complement and enhance the staff—someone who is committed to the objectives of the school and willing to work persistently and collaboratively with others to achieve those goals.
- There is no single curriculum that is evident in these schools, but rather a set of common characteristics. At the core of this is a rich and coherent curriculum based on the state standards, with high expectations for all students. Data are embraced by the staff and used to hold themselves accountable, and to continually examine their practice.
- Systems and structures are in place to ensure the success of all students. There is a certain rhythm in each of these schools—a routine that students and faculty can count on to plan their day and use their time wisely. They realize that time is a valuable commodity not to be wasted, and they pack as much instructional time into the day as possible. Many of these schools have set aside blocks of time for uninterrupted instruction during the day so that teachers and students are completely focused on learning. A variety of academic supports are in place to assist and support the struggling student. It may be with a longer school day, extended instruction before or after the school day, or summer sessions. It could also be with individual tutoring, the help of an aide, or a "big brother." There is an atmosphere of caring, support, and respect for students in these schools.
- Collaborative leadership and professionalism are practiced in these schools. Students, parents, and teachers are highly regarded and treated with respect. All opinions are valued and taken into account when decisions are made. Distributive leadership is welcomed and encouraged by the principal. A well-planned, comprehensive professional-development program is key to the ongoing effort to improve learning for all students. Teachers are provided with various opportunities to improve their skills, i.e., (a) time to observe each other, (b) time to meet and plan with colleagues, and

(c) time to attend conferences and/or workshops. Professional development is a critical component to the school's ability to attain its mission.
- These schools do not operate in a vacuum. They realize that they are microcosms of the greater community. As such, many of the schools have developed partnerships with community organizations and institutions such as neighboring businesses, public agencies, chambers of commerce, and universities. These partnerships have proven to be mutually beneficial. In some cases students have been able to intern in the partner organization or business, allowing students life experiences that broaden their horizons of the future.
- The family and community are integral to the success of these schools. In many instances the school serves as a focus for the neighborhood. Some schools have an actual family center on campus that provides varied services to parents, including educational classes, counseling services, temporary assistance, and referrals to meet basic needs. Schools that have limited space provide a location for parents and community members to meet and participate in school activities. Parents and community members are welcomed and seen as valuable resources at these schools.

In conclusion, the schools discussed here have faced the same obstacles that many of our urban schools encounter, such as high poverty, violence, low student expectations, and low student achievement. In spite of these challenges these schools have broken down the barriers to learning and are achieving great success because of their unwavering dedication and tireless efforts. These educational pioneers are providing a guiding light for the future of urban schools.

References

Center on Educational Governance. (2013). *USC/school performance dashboard/interactive report.* Retrieved on August 28, 2013, from http://www.usc.edu/dept/education/cegov/products/csi-interactive/index.html

City Academy High School. (n.d.). Retrieved on August 27, 2013, from http://en.wikipedia.org/wiki/City_Academy_High_School

Clayton, S. (2008). *Analysis of the 1989 teacher strike: UTLA and LAUSD.* Claremont, CA: Claremont Graduate University.

Collins, J. (2001). *Good to great: Why some companies make the leap . . . and others don't.* New York: Harper Collins.

Danielson, C. (2007). *Enhancing professional practice: A framework for teaching.* Alexandria, VA: Association for Supervision and Curriculum Development.

Kerchner, C. T., Menefee-Libey, D. J., Mulfinger, L. S., & Clayton, S. E. (2008). *Learning from L.A.: Institutional change in American public education.* Cambridge, MA: Harvard Education Press.

Los Angeles Unified School District. (n.d.). Retrieved on March 10, 2014, from home.lausd.net/apps/pages/index.jsp?uRec_ID=178745&type=d&pREC_ID=371201)

Marzano, R. J., Frontier, T., & Livingston, D. (2011). *Effective supervision: Supporting the art and science of teaching.* Alexandria, VA: Association for Supervision and Curriculum Development.

Marzano, R. J., Pickering, D. J., & Pollock, J. E. (2001). *Classroom instruction that works: Research-based strategies for increasing student achievement.* Alexandria, VA: Association for Supervision and Curriculum Development.

Minnesota Department of Education. (2013). *Charter schools.* Retrieved on August 28, 2013, from http://www.education.state.mn.us/MDE/StuSuc/EnrollChoice/CharterSch

National Commission on Excellence in Education. (1983). *A nation at risk: The imperative for educational reform.* Washington, DC: United States Department of Education.

Ouchi, William. (1999, May). Education reform lessons learned from the trenches. *Cal-Tax Digest.* Retrieved on September 10, 2013, from http://caltax.org/MEMBER/digest/May99/may99-3.htm

Staff. (2011, September 2). A weaker Public School Choice initiative. *Los Angeles Times.* Retrieved on September 10, 2013, from http://articles.latimes.com/2011/sep/02/opinion/la-ed-school-20110902

Index

Academic Performance Index (API): of AMLA, 16–17, *17*; of Bright Star, 78, *78*; of Camino Nuevo, 121, *121*; of DOMHS, *98*, 99, 100; of ESAT, 89, *89*; of Fenton, 5, *5*; of GCS, *131*, 132; of Lakeview, *49*; of Larchmont, 141, *141*; of Magnolia Schools, 157; of Milagro, 25, *25*; of MSA-1, *151*; of OCS, 161, *161*; of POLAHS, *108*, 109; of Synergy, 34–35, *35*; of Valor, 59, *59*, 65; of View Park, 68, *69*; of VNCLC, *171*, 172

Accord Institute, 151

accountability: of faculty and staff, 6, 7–8, 12–13, 78, 116, 174–75, 182; of students, 11, 12–13, 57, 79, 82, 83

admissions, xxiv; at Camino Nuevo, 121; at Fenton, 4; at GCS, 131; at Lakeview, 48; at Larchmont, 139; at Milagro, 25; at OCS, 160; at Valor, 58

Advanced Placement (AP), 90, 99–100, 102, 150

Advancement Via Individual Determination program (AVID), 91

Aeries program, 84, 109, 114

after-school programs: of AMLA, 19; of DOMHS, 102–3; of GCS, 129–30; of Lakeview, 50; of MSA-1, 152–53; of POLAHS, 109, 113; of View Park, 70, 71, 72, 74

Albion Elementary, 24–25

Alliance for College Ready Public Schools, xvi; DOMHS as, 97, 100–102, 104; ESAT as, 87–88, 93, 95; philosophy of, 97; responsibilities of, 88

AMLA. *See* Antonio Maria Lugo Academy

AMOs. *See* Annual Measurable Objectives

animals, 163–64

Annenberg, Walter, xxiii

Annual Measurable Objectives (AMOs): Fenton and, *5*, 5–6; GCS and, *131*, 132; Larchmont and, 141, *141*; VNCLC and, *171*, 172

Antonio Maria Lugo Academy (AMLA), xiv; academic accomplishments of, 17–18; as Aspire Public School, 15; Common Core at, 19; community at, 21, 22; CST and, 17–18; data on, 16–17, *17*; future plans of, 21–22; leadership at, 16, 30–31; parental involvement at, 21; professional development at, 20; special programs of, 19–20, 21; success factors of, 18–21
AP. *See* Advanced Placement
API. *See* Academic Performance Index
Apple TV, 20
Aspire Public Schools, xiv; AMLA as, 15; as charter management organization, 15–16; core values of, 16; data analysis of, 17–18; Data Drivers and, 18; mission of, 15–16; professional development within, 20; special programs of, 19–20
assessments, standards-based, 109
AVID. *See* Advancement Via Individual Determination program
Axelrad, Gabriella, 129

behavior and discipline: at Bright Star, 83; at Fenton, 11; at GCS, 133, 134; at Lakeview, 52–53; at MSA-1, 156, 158; for SDC students, 9; SLANT and, 134; at Synergy, 39–40; at Valor, 63; at Vaughn, 176; at View Park, 72
behavior specialist, 9
Benjamin, Roberta, 16, 17–21
Bercovici, Liza, 129–30, 133, 135–36, 137

bilingual programs, 123
bilingual students, 4–5, 27–28
bilingual teachers, 3, 28, 169, 170
Bill and Melinda Gates Foundation, 20, 30, 93, 101
Blending Learning for Alliance School Transformation (BLEND), 88
Bonilla, Monique, 79, 85
Boro, Jessica, 63, 65, 66
Bright Star Academy, xv; achievements of, 77–78; behavior and discipline at, 83; college preparedness of, 80–81, 82, 84–85; community service and, 82; data on, *78*, 78–79; expectations at, 78–80, 85; future plans of, 84; graduation requirements of, 81–82; parental involvement at, 84; reading requirements at, 82; social promotion at, 79–80, 85; special programs of, 80–81, 82–83, 84; success factors of, 80–83; support for students at, 81, 83, 84
Bright Star charter organization, 65, 77
budget cuts, 7, 50, 167
Building Excellent Schools program, 58
Burton, Judy, 88

CAHSEE. *See* California High School Exit Exam
California Academy for Liberal Studies Middle School (CALS), 47
California Association for Gifted teaching strategies, 50
California Charter School Association, 159–60

California Distinguished School Award, 24, 42, 59, 78, 121, 171
California High School Exit Exam (CAHSEE), 81, 109, 150
California Standards Tests (CST): and AMLA, 17–18; and Camino Nuevo, 121; and GCS, 132; and Lakeview, 50; and Larchmont, 147–48; and Milagro, 25–26; and MSA-1, 151; and OCS, 161, 162; and POLAHS, 109; and View Park, 69
California State University Northridge (CSUN), 52
Calkins, Lucy, 19, 27, 144
CALS. *See* California Academy for Liberal Studies Middle School
Camino Nuevo Charter Academy, xvi; achievements of, 121; college preparedness of, 120, 124; Common Core at, 122; as community-based school, 119–20, 122, 126, 127; CST and, 121; data on, 120–21, *121*, 122; English language development at, 123–24; enrichment opportunities at, 125–26, 127; future plans of, 126; hiring protocol of, 123; Home Support Office of, 120; leadership at, 119–20, 122, 127; optimistic views of, 127; parental involvement at, 122, 125–26; professional development at, 122, 123, 124, 127; special programs of, 123–24, 125–26; start of, 119; success factors of, 122–26; support at, 123, 124, 127
Camino Nuevo Charter organization, 120

Camino Nuevo Teachers Association, 120
CARES model, 21
Center for Math and Science Teachers program (CMAST), 102
charter elementary schools, xiv. *See also* Antonio Maria Lugo Academy; Fenton Avenue Charter School; Milagro Charter School; Synergy Charter Academy
charter high schools, xv–xvi. *See also* Bright Star Academy; Dr. Olga Mohan High School; Environmental Science and Technology High School; Port of Los Angeles High School
charter management organization, xiv, 15–16
charter middle schools, xiv–xv. *See also* Lakeview Charter Academy; Valor Academy Middle School; View Park Preparatory Charter Middle School
charter petition, 4–5, 10
charter schools: flexibility in, 80, 93, 100, 111, 150; growth of, xxii; legislation in, xxi–xxii; movement, xiii, xxi–xxiv
charter span schools, xvi–xvii. *See also* Camino Nuevo Charter Academy; Gabriella Charter School; Larchmont Charter School; Magnolia Science Academy; Our Community School; Vaughn Next Century Learning Center
City Academy High School, xxi
Classroom Instruction That Works (Marzano), 8–9
Close Reading, 72

CMAST. *See* Center for Math and Science Teachers program
cognitive strategies, 8
COI. *See* Cycle of Inquiry
collaborative colocation strategy, 34, 38–39
college preparedness: of Bright Star Academy, 80–81, 82, 84–85; of Camino Nuevo Charter Academy, 120, 124; of DOMHS, 99, 105; of LA charter schools, 181; of MSA-1, 154–55, 158; of POLAHS, 114; of Valor, 60–61, 65, 66; of View Park, 71, 74. *See also* Alliance for College Ready Public Schools; The College-Ready Promise
Common Core: at AMLA, 19; at Camino Nuevo, 122; at DOMHS, 101; at Milagro, 27–28, 31; at Synergy, 36, 37; at View Park, 73
community: at AMLA, 21, 22; at Camino Nuevo, 119–20, 122, 126, 127; Larchmont and, 140, 145, 147; MSA-1 at, 154–55, 157; at OCS, 164, 165, 167, 168; partnerships, 64, 167, 183; at Valor, 63–64; VNCLC at, 171, 172, 178
Community Charter Middle School, 24, 47, 48
Community Circle, 63
community service, 53, 73, 82, 91, 103
community support, at Los Angeles charter schools, 183
Concept 6 multitrack calender, 169
Connecting Place (CP), 83, 84
constructivist-based learning, 38, 134–35, 139–40, 141–43, 147, 148

conversion charters, xiv, xvi–xvii, xxiv, 4, 170–71
CoolSIS, 155–56, 158
core curriculum, 9
Cornell Note-taking, 72
counseling services: academic, 68, 94, 103, 113; family related, 11, 21, 72, 125, 127, 178, 183
CP. *See* Connecting Place
Critical Friends concept, 73
CST. *See* California Standards Tests
CSUN. *See* California State University Northridge
culminative study, 144–45, 163–64
Culver City Unified School District, 149
curriculum, standards-based, 21, 71, 73, 132–33, 135, 166
Cycle of Inquiry (COI), 18

dance, 129, 132–33
Danielson, Charlotte, 175
DAP. *See* differentiated action plan
data analysis: of Aspire Public Schools, 17–18; at Camino Nuevo, 122; at DOMHS, 101; at Fenton, 9–10, 13; at Larchmont, 143; at Milagro, 29; at OCS, 162–63, 168; at POLAHS, 109, 112–13; at View Park, 70
Data Director, 48, 80, 109, 112–13, 122, 162
decision making: shared, xxii, 12, 13, 172; site-based, 111
demographics: of AMLA, 17; of Bright Star, 78; of Camino Nuevo, 122; of DOMHS, 99; of Milagro, 24–25; of OCS, 159; of VNCLC, 169

differentiated action plan (DAP), 60, 66
discipline. *See* behavior and discipline
Dr. Olga Mohan High School (DOMHS), xvi; college preparedness of, 99, 105; Common Core at, 101; community service and, 103; data on, *98*, 98–100, 101–2; empowerment at, 97; English learners at, 101–2; freedom in leadership at, 100, 105; fund-raising at, 102; future plans of, 104; hiring at, 101; parental involvement at, 103; partnerships of, 102–3; professional development at, 101; special programs of, 99, 101–3; standards-based grading system at, 100, 104, 105; student activities at, 102; success factors of, 99, 100–103; teacher resources at, 101
dual enrollment, 81, 91
Dweck, Carol, 27

educational reform, xxi
educational reform movement, xiii–xiv
EL. *See* English learners
ELA. *See* English language arts
Elliot, Jacquelin, xv, 24, 47
empowerment, 125–26; of staff, 12–13, 16, 22, 49; of students, 11, 12–13, 27, 37, 165
English language arts (ELA), 60, 61, 132
English learners (EL), 51, 92, 170
Enhancing Professional Practice: A Framework for Teaching (Danielson), 175

Environmental Science and Technology High School (ESAT), xvi; community service and, 91; core education model of, 90; data on, 88–90, *89*; expectations at, 91, 92, 95; future plans of, 94; hiring at, 92–93; leadership at, 91, 94, 95; parental involvement at, 94; professional development at, 92–93; special programs of, 91–92, 93; success factors of, 90–94; sustainability of, 88; testing at, 90
EPK. *See* extending prior knowledge
Epps, Jennifer, 34–40
ESAT. *See* Environmental Science and Technology High School
ESLRs. *See* Expected Schoolwide Learning Results
Everybody Dance! program, 129
Excel, 153
expectations: of faculty and staff, 92, 138, 143, 175–77; of parents, 71, 133–34, 136–37; of students, 12–13, 63, 78–80, 85, 91–92, 95, 132–34, 138, 145, 182
Expected Schoolwide Learning Results (ESLRs), 146

faculty. *See* faculty and staff
faculty and staff: accountability of, 6, 7–8, 12–13, 78, 116, 174–75, 182; empowerment of, 12–13, 16, 22, 49; expectations of, 92, 138, 143, 175–77; freedom of, 150; passion of, 174; pay incentives of, 179; preparation of, 175–76; resources for, 136; support of, 63, 66, 110–13, 123, 136, 173, 174
family support services, 21, 127, 145, 178, 183

feedback, 145
Fenton Avenue Charter School, xiv; AMOs and, 5, 5–6; behavior and discipline at, 11; bilingualism at, 3, 4–5; challenges of, 3; as conversion charter, 4; data on, 5, 5–6, 8; as elementary school, 5; faculty and staff of, 6–7, 12–13; funding of, 7; future plans of, 11–12; governance model of, 6–7; growth of students at, 10–11; hiring and firing at, 7–8; LAUSD and, 3, 12; leadership at, 6–7, 12–13; mission of, 10–11; as primary center, 5; professional development at, 8, 13; professionalism at, 12; Program Improvement and, 6; Safe Harbor and, 6; special programs of, 5, 6, 9, 11; success factors of, 6–11; technology and, 10
Ferris, Christine, 159–62
flexibility, 80, 93, 100, 111, 150
Foshay Middle School, 87
Four Pillars, 110–12
fund-raising, 7, 21, 30, 70, 102, 167

Gabriella Axelrad Foundation, 129
Gabriella Charter School (GCS), xvi; achievements of, 130; AMOs and, *131*, 132; behavior and discipline at, 133, 134; colocation and, 130–31; constructivist-based learning at, 134–35; CST and, 132; as dance-themed school, 129, 132–33; data on, *131*, 131–32; expectations of students at, 132–34, 138; feedback and, 135, 137; freedom and motivation of staff at, 130; future plans of, 137; high-performing mentality of, 130; hiring at, 135–36, 138; motivation of students at, 138; parental involvement at, 136–37, 138; professional development at, 135; special programs of, 129–30, 132–33; standards-based curriculum at, 132–33, 135; start of, 129; support at, 136, 137; teamwork and, 133
Get Ready For Life (GRFL) curriculum, 153–54
governance structures, 6–7, 12, 71, 172–73, 178, 179
grading, standards-based, 79, 100, 104, 105
grants, 47, 107
GRFL. *See* Get Ready For Life

Hamalian, Hrag, xv, 57–58, 60, 62–66
handwriting, 146
Herrick Avenue, 177
Hilger, Jeff, xv, 77, 80–82, 84
hiring: at Camino Nuevo, 123; at DOMHS, 101; at ESAT, 92–93; at Fenton, 7; at GCS, 135–36, 138; at LA charter schools, 182; at Lakeview, 54–55; at Larchmont, 145–46, 148; at OCS, 166; at Synergy, 38, 43; at View Park, 71; at VNCLC, 174
Holiday, Sean, 119–20, 122, 124
Hollygrove Children and Family Services, 140–41
Huntington Park, 15, 21–22

ICEF. *See* Inner City Education Foundation
IEP. *See* Individualized Education Program

INDEX 193

inclusion specialist, 51
Individualized Education Program (IEP), 51, 145
Inner City Education Foundation (ICEF): College Readiness Model of, 67–68, 69, 71; Piscal, Michael, as founder of, xv, 67
interdisciplinary study, 143–44
international studies, 171
iPad, 20
I-Station, 10

Jackson, Kenya, 68–74

Kaplan, Sandra, 50
Keene, Ellin, 27
Khan Academy, 152
Killbourn, Martha, 58, 61, 66
KIPP. *See* Knowledge is Power Program
Knowledge is Power Program (KIPP), 58, 77, 93

LAAMP. *See* Los Angeles Annenberg Metropolitan Project
Lakeview Charter Academy, xiv–xv; behavior and discipline at, 52–53; community service and, 53; CST and, 50; data on, 48–49, *49*, 56; future plans of, 54, 55; hiring protocol at, 54–55; professional development at, 48–49; PUC commitments at, 55; routines and procedures of, 53, 56; special programs of, 50–52, 55, 56; success factors of, 50–55; teacher development-systems of, 54
Lance, Philip, 119
Lappin, Howard, 87, 88, 91–94

Larchmont Charter School, xvi; AMOs and, 141, *141*; community and, 140, 145, 147; constructivist-based learning at, 139–40, 141–43, 147, 148; CST and, 147–48; curriculum maps of, 145; data on, 141, *141*, 141–42, 146; diversity of, 139–40, 142; ESLRs and, 146; expectations at, 143, 145; feedback at, 145; future plans of, 147; grade-level configuration at, 140; handwriting at, 146; hiring at, 145–46, 148; Hollygrove Children and Family Services and, 140; interdisciplinary study at, 143–44; metaphors and, 146; philosophy of, 141–43, *142*; professional development at, 146; Readers and Writers Workshop and, 144–45; special programs of, 142; success factors of, 142–46; WASC Action Plan, 147
LAUSD. *See* Los Angeles Unified School District
leadership, 112; at AMLA, 16, 30–31; at Camino Nuevo, 119–20, 122, 127; collaborative, 71, 73–74, 145, 182; distributive, 6–7, 12–13, 171–72, 182; at DOMHS, 101, 105; at ESAT, 91, 94, 95; at Fenton, 6–7, 12–13; at LA charter schools, 182; at POLAHS, 112; at VNCLC, 171–72
Leadership in Energy and Environmental Design (LEED), 88
lead teachers, 8, 101, 110–13, 116
LEARN. *See* Los Angeles Educational Alliance for Restructuring Now

Learning Lab, 51
LEED. *See* Leadership in Energy and Environmental Design
Life Experience Lessons (LELs), 82
Lincoln Heights Neighborhood Council, 30–31
Logan Street Elementary School, 130–31
Los Angeles Annenberg Metropolitan Project (LAAMP), xxiii, 87
Los Angeles charter schools: can-do culture of, 181; challenges of, 181, 183; college preparedness of, 181; expectations of, 182; hiring at, 182; leadership techniques at, 182; professional development at, 182–83; professionalism at, 182; standards of, 182; success of, 181; support of, 182, 183; vision of, 181
Los Angeles Educational Alliance for Restructuring Now (LEARN), xxiii, 87
Los Angeles magazine, 130
Los Angeles school reforms, xiii
Los Angeles Unified School District (LAUSD), xiii–xvi, xxii, xxiv, 17, 170; Board of Education, xxiii, 24; ESAT and, 89–90; Fenton with, 3, 12; requirement mandates of, 48; school reform, xvi, xxii–xxiv, 87; Teach for America and, 57
lottery enrollment. *See* admissions
Lucente, Joe, 3, 7

MacArthur Park, 119
Magnolia Education & Research Foundation, 149, 156–57
Magnolia Science Academy-Reseda (MSA-1), xvi; achievements of, 157; behavior and discipline at, 156, 158; college preparedness of, 154–55, 158; as community-based school, 154–55, 157; computer education, 153, 158; CST and, 151; Culver City Unified School District and, 149; data on, 150–53, *151*; discipline at, 156; electives at, 152; English Learners at, 153; enrichment activities of, 155; enrollment at, *151*; foreign language at, 152; future plans of, 156–57; GRFL curriculum and, 153–54; incentives at, 156; Magnolia Education & Research Foundation and, 149; MAP at, 151–52; parental involvement at, 155–56, 158; Pi Day at, 155; special programs of, 149, 152, 153, 155–56, 157; success factors of, 152–56; support at, 153, 154, 157; university-themed classrooms, 154
MAP. *See* Measures of Academic Progress
Marzano, R. J., 8–9
Measures of Academic Progress (MAP), 151–52
metacognitive, 28
metaphors, 146
Milagro Charter School, xiv; as award winning school, 24; bilingualism at, 27–28; Common Core at, 27–28, 31; CST and, 25–26; curriculum maps of, 27; daily assessment of students at, 26; data on, 24–25, *25*; future

INDEX   195

plans of, 31; parental involvement at, 27, 30; partnership with Pasadena Armory Art Center, 29; professional development at, 29; as PUC school, 23; success factors of, 26–31; technology, need for, 31
Mindset (Dweck), 27
Minnesota, xxi
Moran, Martha, 24, 27–31
MSA-1. *See* Magnolia Science Academy-Reseda
Mutt-i-gree program, 11

National Blue Ribbon Schools Award, 171
A Nation at Risk: The Imperative for Educational Reform, xxi
No Child Left Behind Program, 34, 161
Northwest Evaluation Association, 151–52
Number Strings, 19

Our Community School (OCS), xvi; animal based learning at, 163–64; as Charter School of the Year, 159–60; community and, 164, 165, 167, 168; CST and, 161, 162; data on, 160–61, *161*, 162–63, 168; diversity of, 160; enrichment activities at, 165, 166; future plans of, 167; hiring at, 166; importance of social issues at, 164; location for, 159–60; math program at, 161; parental involvement at, 165–67; partnerships with, 167; Peaceful Learning Communities and, 167, 168; professional development at, 162–63, 168; reading comprehension at, 162; social and emotional development at, 168; special programs of, 161, 165–66; start of, 159; student support at, 162; success factors of, 163–67

Pacific Charter School Development Corporation, 48, 68
Palisoc, Meg, 33–34, 38, 41–42
Palisoc, Randy, 33–36, 38–39, 41–42
Panda Academy, 171
PandaLand, 171
PAR. *See* Peer Assistance and Review
parental involvement: at AMLA, 21; at Bright Star, 84; at Camino Nuevo, 122, 125–26; at DOMHS, 103; at ESAT, 94; at GCS, 136–37, 138; at Milagro, 27, 30; at MSA-1, 155–56, 158; at OCS, 165–67; at Synergy, 40–41; at View Park, 70–71
parental support, of Los Angeles charter schools, 183
parents: expectations of, 71, 133–34, 136–37; support and, 125–26, 137, 178, 183
PAR evaluation process, 174–77, 178, 179
PAR matrix: for apprentice teachers, 175–76; *Enhancing Professional Practice: A Framework for Teaching* and, 175; for K-12, 175, 176–77
partnerships: community, 167; with Los Angeles charter schools, 183; with Los Angeles Harbor College, 114, 115; Loyola

Marymount University and, 102; San Pedro Chamber of Commerce and, 115–16; the Youth Policy Institute and, 102–3
Partnerships to Uplift Communities (PUC), xiv, 23–24, 47–48, 53, 54. *See also* PUC schools
Pasadena Armory Art Center, 29
PASS. *See* Personalized Academic Support Program
PD. *See* professional development
Peaceful Learning Communities (PLC), 165, 167, 168
Pearson's Good Habits Great Readers, 162
Peer Assistance and Review (PAR), 174–79
peer-organized development teams (PODs), 54
*P*ersistence, *O*wnership, *D*esire, *E*mpowerment, and *R*espect (PODER), 125–26
Personalized Academic Support Program (PASS), 113, 116
Personnel Committee, 174
Pi Day, 155
Piscal, Michael, xv, 67
PLC. *See* Peaceful Learning Communities
PODER. *See P*ersistence, *O*wnership, *D*esire, *E*mpowerment, and *R*espect
PODs. *See* peer-organized development teams
POLAHS. *See* Port of Los Angeles High School
Ponce, Manuel, Jr., 48–50, 51–52, 54
Port of Los Angeles, 116
Port of Los Angeles High School (POLAHS), xvi; college preparedness of, 114; CST and, 109; culture of, 108; data on, *108*, 109, 112–13; as Distinguished School, 116; Four Pillars of, 110–12; future plans of, 115; graduation requirements of, 113, 114; grant for, 107; leadership structure of, 112; lead teachers at, 110–12, 116; partnerships with, 114, 115–16; PASS and, 116; professional development at, 111–13, 115; professionalism at, 108, 112, 116; special programs of, 109–10, 113–14, 115–16; start-up of, 107; students of, 113–14, 115–16; success factors of, 110–14; support of staff at, 110–13; technology and, 114
Power Over Numbers, 36, 37, 39, 43
Power Over Words, 36, 39, 43
PREP. *See* Prepared, Respectful, Engaged, and Professional
Prepared, Respectful, Engaged, and Professional (PREP), 62–63, 65
prep year, 81, 85
professional development (PD): at AMLA, 20; at Camino Nuevo, 122, 123, 124, 127; *Classroom Instruction That Works* (Marzano) and, 8–9; at DOMHS, 101; at ESAT, 92–93; at Fenton, 8, 13; at GCS, 135; at Lakeview, 48–49; at Larchmont, 146; at Los Angeles charter schools, 182–83; at Milagro, 29; at OCS, 162–63, 168; at POLAHS, 111–13, 115; at Synergy, 35, 39, 41; at Valor, 62;

at Vaughn, 173; at View Park, 72, 74
professionalism: at Fenton, 12; at LA charter schools, 182; at POLAHS, 108, 112, 116; at Valor, 63–65; at View Park, 73
project-based learning, 134, 140, 142, 148, 164, 167
PSC. *See* Public School Choice
Public School Choice (PSC), xxiv
PUC. *See* Partnerships to Uplift Communities
PUC charter school development and management corporation, 47–48
PUC schools, 23–24, 30, 48, 50–55
The Purple Planet, 20–21

Quincy Jones Elementary School, 34, 38–39

RC. *See* Responsive Classrooms
Readers and Writers Workshop, 19, 144–45
reading comprehension, 28; Pearson's Good Habits Great Readers, 162; Words Their Way, 162
Reading Counts, 36–37, 43, 82
recess, 36, 39
resource specialist teacher (RST), 9, 101
Response to Intervention (RtI), 10, 19
Responsive Classrooms (RC), 164, 167, 168
Riddick, David, 7, 9, 12
Robinett, Sascha, 24, 27–31
Rodriguez, Janette, 97–98, 100–104

Rodriguez, Ref, xv, 24, 47
Rooney, Lisa, 130, 133
RST. *See* resource specialist teacher
RtI. *See* Response to Intervention

Safe Harbor, 6, 132, 141, 161, 172
San Pedro Chamber of Commerce, 115–16
Saturday school, 21, 50, 70, 114, 152, 156
SBM. *See* school-based management
Scholar Success Center, 51
school-based management (SBM), xxii, 170
science, technology, engineering, and mathematics (STEM), 34, 149, 178
SDC. *See* special day class
SDM. *See* shared-decision making
self-segregation, 139–40
shared-decision making (SDM), xxii 12, 13, 172
Singapore Math, 122, 124, 161
SLANT, 134
slow-growth model, 65
SLS. *See* Student-Led Solution
social and emotional development, 168
social and emotional skills, 11
special day class (SDC), 9
special education, 9, 135, 142, 153–54
special programs: Aeries, 84, 109, 114; Bill and Melinda Gates Foundation, 20, 93, 101; CMAST and, 102; dance programs, 129, 132–33; internships, 113, 115–16; Khan Academy, 152; PASS as, 113; Singapore Math, 124, 161;

Teachers College Reading and Writing program, 124; Ultimate Transformations, 72; The Youth Policy Institute, 72. *See also specific schools*
staff. *See* faculty and staff
standardized testing and reporting (STAR), 59, 69, 70, 79
STAR. *See* standardized testing and reporting
start-up challenges, xiv, xxiv, 4, 33–34, 41–42
STEM. *See* science, technology, engineering, and mathematics
Step Up To Writing, 36, 43
structured systems, 62, 182
student interaction, 28
Student-Led Solution (SLS), 20
students: accountability of, 11, 12–13, 57, 79, 82, 83; assessment of, 26, 136, 143, 148; bilingual, 4–5, 27–28; empowerment of, 11, 12–13, 27, 37, 165; expectations of, 12–13, 63, 78–80, 85, 91–92, 95, 132–34, 138, 145, 182; growth of, 10, 26; routines and procedures for, 53, 56; struggles of, 124; support of, 26, 31, 51, 81, 83, 84, 102–3, 124, 126, 127, 145, 153, 157, 162, 173–74
Study Island, 51, 61, 69, 79
Sumida, Irene, 3, 7
support: parents and, 125–26, 137, 178, 183; of staff, 63, 66, 110–13, 123, 136, 173, 174; of students, 26, 31, 51, 81, 83, 84, 102–3, 124, 126, 127, 145, 153, 157, 162, 173–74
supportive relationships, 97

Synergy Charter Academy, xiv, 33; accomplishments of, 36, 42; behavior and discipline at, 39–40; collaborative colocation strategy and, 34, 38–39; Common Core at, 36, 37; data on, 34–35, *35*; discipline at, 39–40; future plans of, 41; hiring at, 38, 43; mathematics strategies at, 36, 37; parental involvement at, 40–41; professional development at, 35, 39, 41; reading strategies of, 36–37; recess structure of, 38; special programs of, 34–35; start-up challenges of, 33–34, 41–42; success factors of, 36–41
Synergy's Scholar Lessons, 39–40
Synergy Trade Secrets Tours, 41

TCRP. *See* The College-Ready Promise
teacher-development system, 54
Teacher-Effectiveness Framework, 53–54, 56
teacher evaluation, 101, 111–13, 162–63, 168, 174–77, 179
teachers. *See* faculty and staff
Teachers' College Reading and Writing program, 124, 144
teacher strike (1989), xxii
teacher union, 120
Teach for America, xv, 57, 77, 120, 123, 130
teaching, standards-based, 79
technology, 10, 31, 149, 153, 158, 178
Technology Integrated Education (TIE©), 153, 158
Teen Biz, 51

The College-Ready Promise (TCRP), 20, 30, 71, 93, 101
Thinking Maps, 6, 8–9, 177
TIE©. *See* Technology Integrated Education
tutoring, 182; at Bright Star, 80; at MSA-1, 149, 152, 153; at POLAHS, 113–14, 116; at Valor, 60

Ultimate Transformations, 72
uniforms: at Bright Star, 78; at ESAT, 91; at Lakeview, 52; at OCS, 167; at Synergy, 39; at Valor, 58; at View Park, 73
United States Academic Decathlon, xiii
University of Southern California (USC), 33, 50
University Park Campus School, 23
University Prep Program (UP), 82
USC. *See* University of Southern California

Valley Community Charter Schools (VCCS), 159
Valor Academy Middle School, xv, 57; achievements of, 65–66; behavioral expectations at, 63; California Distinguished School Award and, 59; college-ready culture of, 60–61, 65, 66; community and, 63–64; data on, 58–60, *59*, 65; future plans of, 64–65; mathematics and, 61; PREP at, 65; professional development of, 62; professionalism at, 63–65; slow-growth model at, 65; structured systems of, 62; Student Ambassador program at, 63–64; success factors of, 60–64; success of students at, 66; teacher support at, 63, 66
Vaughn Next Century Learning Center (VNCLC), xvi; achievements of, 171; admission preferences of, 170–71; AMOs and, *171*, 172; behavior and discipline at, 176; bilingual teachers at, 169, 170; challenges of, 169–70; as community based charter school, 171, 172, 178; data on, *171*, 172; distributive leadership model and, 171–72; enrichment at, 171, 172–73; ethnic balance, change of, 169; expectations of teachers at, 175–77; financial management at, 174; frustrations with LAUSD, 170; as full-service facility, 179; future plans of, 177–78; governance structure of, 172–73, 178, 179; growth of, 171; hiring at, 174; jobs created by, 178; PAR and, 174–77, 178, 179; passion of teachers at, 174, 178; pay incentives at, 177; Personnel Committee at, 174; professional development at, 173; as Program Improvement 5 school, 172; responsibilities of teachers at, 176; school-based health clinic at, 178; special services of, 178; success factors of, 172–77; support at, 173–74, 178; teacher preparation at, 175–76; technology at, 178; Thinking Maps at, 177; trust at, 173

VCCS. *See* Valley Community Charter Schools

View Park Preparatory Charter Middle School: achievements of, 67, 73, 74; behavior and discipline at, 72; challenges of, 68–69; college-ready culture of, 71, 74; Common Core at, 73; Critical Friends concept and, 73; CST and, 69; data on, 68–69, *69*, 70; future plans of, 73–74; hiring/firing at, 71; ICEF and, xv, 67–68, 69, 71; mentoring/counseling services of, 72; parental involvement at, 70–71; professional development at, 72, 74; professionalism at, 73; rewards at, 73; special programs at, 70, 71, 72, 74; success factors of, 70–73; teaching strategies at, 71–72; testing at, 69–70

VNCLC. *See* Vaughn Next Century Learning Center

volunteers, 21

WASC Action Plan, 147
Water Day, 42
Words Their Way, 162
world languages, 171

The Youth Policy Institute, 72, 102–3

About the Authors

Joseph Scollo, the project lead of this study, has over forty-five years of experience as a teacher, school principal, director of curriculum and instruction, adjunct professor, doctoral program coordinator, and full-time lecturer. He served as a writer and codirector for the Urban School Leaders program and the Charter and Autonomous School Leadership Academy at California State University Dominguez Hills. These programs were funded by two multiyear, multimillion-dollar grants awarded by the United States Department of Education School Leadership Department. Joe holds a master of arts degree in educational administration from California State University Long Beach and a doctorate of education in school leadership from Nova Southeastern University.

Dona Stevens served as principal researcher and author for this study. Her twenty-eight years of experience include teacher, school principal, administrator of instruction, interim superintendent, and adjunct professor. She holds a master of arts degree from California State University Dominguez Hills and a doctorate of education in school leadership from Nova Southeastern University.

Ellen Pomella worked as a researcher and author for this study. Her career spanned thirty-seven years in secondary education, serving as a teacher, counselor, instructional coach, assistant principal, and district administrator. She earned her master of arts degree from California State University Dominguez Hills, and currently works as a consultant for the Los Angeles School Development Institute creating and implementing plans to improve schools.

www.ingramcontent.com/pod-product-compliance
Lightning Source LLC
Chambersburg PA
CBHW030111010526
44116CB00005B/192